Gardening
Month by Month
in Illinois

William Aldrich & Don Williamson

Lone Pine Publishing

The Publisher: Lone Pine Publishing

10145 – 81 Avenue
Edmonton, AB T6E 1W9 Canada
Website: www.lonepinepublishing.com

1808 B Street NW, Suite 140
Auburn, WA, USA 98001

National Library of Canada Cataloguing in Publication

Aldrich, William, 1948-
  Month by month gardening in Illinois / William Aldrich, Don Williamson.

  ISBN 1-55105-375-6

  1. Gardening—Illinois—Calendars. 2. Gardening—Illinois.
I. Williamson, Don, 1962- II. Title.
SB453.2.I3A43 2004   635'.09773   C2003-907160-X

Editorial Director: Nancy Foulds
Project Editor: Sandra Bit
Researchers: Don Williamson, Laura Peters
Production Manager: Gene Longson
Book Design, Layout & Production: Heather Markham
Maps & Climate Charts: Elliot Engley, Chia-Jung Chang
Cover Design: Gerry Dotto
Principal Photographers: Tamara Eder, Tim Matheson
Illustrations: Ian Sheldon
Scanning, Separations & Film: Elite Lithographers Co.

Front cover photographs by Tamara Eder except where noted. Clockwise from top left, outer circle: daylily (*Tim Matheson*), golden marguerite, dahlia (*Tim Matheson*), climbing rose 'Laura Ford', daylily (*Tim Matheson*), garden sage, climbing rose 'Laura Ford', heliopsis; centre, shrub rose 'Morden Sunrise'

The photographs in this book are reproduced with the generous permission of their copyright holders.

All other photos: All-American Selections 99c, 120–121; Sandra Bit 35b, 75b&c, 81a; Linda Oyama Bryan 4–5, 7a, 35a, 35d, 75a&d; Therese D'Monte 70; Don Doucette 15a, 23b, 39c, 147a&b; Elliot Engley 31b&d, 33a&b; Jennifer Fafard123c, 125b&c, 127a&b, 129c, 131a&b, 132–33, 137b, 151b, 155c; Erika Flatt 35e; Anne Gordon 137c; Saxon Holt 31a, 111b, 148; Horticolor©Nova-Photographik/Horticolor 94; Colin Laroque 96–97; Heather Markham 57b, 117b; Marilynn McAra 36–37, 43b,c&d, 51c, 115a&d; Kim O'Leary 29b, 111a, 149a; Alison Penko 113c; Laura Peters 17a, 35c, 79a, 119c, 147c, 149d, 151a&c, 153c, 155a&b; Robert Ritchie 59a, 139a; Peter Thompstone 45b, 105a, 141a; Don Williamson 19a&b, 27b, 119a, 135b, 144–45

Frost dates maps: data provided by the Illinois State Climatologist's Office, a part of the Illinois State Water Survey (ISWS) located in Champaign, Peoria, Carbondale, and Chicago, Illinois, (www.sws.uiuc.edu/atmos/statecli); *Hardiness zones map:* based on the USDA Plant Hardiness Zones Map; *Climate normals and extremes charts:* data from the National Oceanic and Atmospheric Administration National Climate Data Center, Asheville, NC (http://mrcc.sws.uiuc.edu/html/MWclimate_data_summaries.htm).

This book is not intended as a 'how-to' guide for eating garden plants. No plant or plant extract should be consumed unless you are certain of its identity and toxicity and of your potential for allergic reactions.

We acknowledge the financial support of the Government of Canada through the Book Publishing Industry Development Program (BPIDP) for our publishing activities.

PC: 01

INTRODUCTION

Gardening is a 365-day-a-year activity. If you only garden from Mother's Day to Labor Day, you are missing a great opportunity. It's not something you have to do everyday, but there is something interesting available to do each and every day.

After reviewing the hints in this volume, I feel as if I'm having a bad dream—yes, I know I need to do all these things, but just where do I find the time and energy to do them all? It's no worse than what many of us go through with other daily tasks, starting off with one chore only to find that one is connected to another that needs doing before the first one can get started, but oh, isn't it more fun to mosey off and do something different instead? This handy guide will help you mosey into your garden and know what to do when you get there.

Gently rolling, fertile plains dominate the natural geography of Illinois, from the lowland flats around Lake Michigan to the hills and valleys in the northwest down to the northern edge of the Shawnee Hills. This vast area is what gave Illinois the name 'The Prairie State.' The Shawnee Hills region, which includes the Shawnee National Forest, is an area of hills, valleys and hardwood forest. To the south of the Shawnee Hills, in Illinois' deep south, is the northern tip of the Gulf Coastal Plain. This area is also known as Little Egypt, for its resemblance to the Nile delta.

The glaciers of the last ice age are primarily responsible for the diverse deposits of soil in Illinois. In fact, around 90% of Illinois is covered by rich, glacier-deposited soil.

Because Illinois is a long state from north to south, gardeners in Rockford may feel as if they have nothing in common with gardeners in Cairo. A stroll through a garden in each city would probably show how wrong this idea is. Many of the same plants will grow in gardens all over Illinois.

violas

Though many books still reflect the presumed hardiness of certain plants, many gardening catalogs and garden centers are beginning to give gardeners a more accurate picture of what will grow here. Many plants that were previously declared 'out of zone' are now known to be hardy in many Illinois gardens. Every imaginable style of garden can be created here, from informal English-style cottage gardens to formal knot gardens. These gardens reflect the style and enthusiasm of their gardeners and the diversity of situations in which they garden.

Where we garden varies almost as much as what we garden. Apartment and condo dwellers enjoy container gardening; rural gardeners may be tilling the same soil that many generations of their ancestors did; urban gardens include those in older neighborhoods with deep topsoil and those whose brand new gardens may have only the thin layer of soil the construction company returned to their yards. Beautiful, successful gardens are possible in every situation, limited only by the imagination of the gardener.

The climate is not without its challenges, and some research and experimentation are required to get the best results from your garden. The short growing season in some northern counties, lack of snowcover, damage caused by ice,

stone path through beds of annuals

heavy rain, snow or wind and possible drought are all climatic challenges gardeners in Illinois face. The key to cold-climate gardening is not how cold it gets, but keeping everything consistently cold. Generally, cycles of freezing and thawing, wet soil and dehydrating winds do more damage than the cold itself. Learning what to expect and when to expect it as well as what plants are best suited to your garden are key elements to gardening anywhere, not just in Illinois.

During the growing season, adequate precipitation can make the difference between gardening success or failure. In a good year, regular rainfall takes care of most of our watering needs and only hanging baskets and beds beneath the overhang of the house need to be

gazanias

bridge pathway (*above*); mini alpine garden (*below*)

naturalistic water feature (*below*)

watered regularly. In a bad year, it seems as if it will never stop raining or that it will never rain again. Although rainfall is fairly dependable, droughts and deluges are always possible. As with all the factors that influence our gardens, we must be prepared to make the most of what nature offers us and try to take up the slack where it lets off.

The length of the growing season also varies greatly. Some northern gardeners have only 160 frost-free days to work with, while some of their southern counterparts enjoy over 200 days between the last and first frost dates. Northern gardens have slightly more hours of sunlight during the summer months, which makes up somewhat for the shorter growing season.

Many of the gardening books available to us are written by and for gardeners who have never done much cold-climate gardening. Most of the general information about gardening is accurate and useful, but hardiness information, for example, is often based on assumption and guess-work and not always on experimentation and knowledge. It is almost always worth trying a plant, even if it isn't supposed to be hardy. It may very well thrive in a sheltered spot in your garden or with an insulating layer of snow.

The purpose of this book is to give you ideas and to help you plan what should be done and when. Garden tasks are listed in the month they should be completed, and general ideas that can be applied in a variety of months are also included. There is plenty of space for you to write in your own thoughts and ideas.

The information in this book is general. If you need more detailed information on a topic, refer to the resources listed at the back of the book. Your local library is also an excellent place to search for the information you need. Gardening courses are offered through colleges, continuing education programs, gardening societies and

mixed border

through Master Gardener programs. You can tackle even the most daunting garden task once you are prepared and well-informed.

Use this book to keep track of unusual weather conditions, when plants sprout and when they first flower. Note the birds and insects you see in the

golden marguerites

garden. If a plant was problematic in a certain location, you will remember not to put it in the same location next year if you add that comment to your book. Jot down your fantastic inspirations for future gardening design plans. You'll appreciate it next spring when memories of this year's garden are getting a little fuzzy.

fountain grass and Wave petunias in a Chicago park

hot peppers

There are no absolute rules when it comes to gardening. No two years are identical, and all information should be taken with a pinch of salt. Use your own best judgment when deciding when to do things in your garden. If spring has been cold and wet you may have to plant later than suggested, or earlier if an early spring warms things up quickly.

Above all else, always take time to enjoy your Illinois garden.

ILLINOIS CLIMATE NORMALS 1971–2000

(Data from the Midwestern Regional Climate Center.)

	CATEGORY	JAN	FEB	MAR	APR	MAY	JUN	JUL	AUG	SEP	OCT	NOV	DEC	YEAR
CARBONDALE	AVG. MAX. TEMP. (°F)	39.3	45.3	55.3	66.2	75.5	84	87.8	86.8	79.9	69.2	55.4	43.8	65.7
	AVG. MIN. TEMP. (°F)	20.8	24.2	33.5	42.4	52.1	61.4	65.9	63.1	55.1	43.3	35	25.6	43.5
	SNOWFALL (IN.)	4.6	3.5	1.8	0.3	0	0	0	0	0	0.1	0.5	2.6	13.4
	*PRECIPITATION (IN.)	2.91	3.01	4.25	4.45	4.78	4.77	3.35	3.94	3.13	2.93	4.62	3.71	45.85
CHICAGO	AVG. MAX. TEMP. (°F)	29.6	34.7	46.1	58	69.9	79.2	83.5	81.2	73.9	62.1	47.1	34.4	58.3
	AVG. MIN. TEMP. (°F)	14.3	19.2	28.5	37.6	47.5	57.2	63.2	62.2	53.7	42.1	31.6	20.4	39.8
	SNOWFALL (IN.)	11.3	8.3	6	1.6	0	0	0	0	0	0.3	1.8	8.7	38
	PRECIPITATION (IN.)	1.75	1.63	2.65	3.68	3.38	3.63	3.51	4.62	3.27	2.71	3.01	2.43	36.27
DANVILLE	AVG. MAX. TEMP. (°F)	34.2	40	52	64.5	75.2	83.5	86.2	84.1	78.4	66.6	51.6	38.7	62.9
	AVG. MIN. TEMP. (°F)	17.3	21.9	31.7	41	50.7	60	64.3	62.6	54.7	43.3	33.8	23	42
	SNOWFALL (IN.)	6.3	4.4	3	0.2	0	0	0	0	0	0.1	1	5.8	20.8
	PRECIPITATION (IN.)	2.05	1.99	3.17	3.86	4.47	4.7	4.39	3.94	3.03	3.04	3.53	2.79	40.96
GALESBURG	AVG. MAX. TEMP. (°F)	29	35.1	47.9	61.2	72.5	81.4	84.5	81.9	74.7	62.7	46.7	33.4	59.3
	AVG. MIN. TEMP. (°F)	13.5	19.2	29.4	40.2	51.4	60.8	65.3	63.2	54.7	42.9	30.8	19.2	40.9
	SNOWFALL (IN.)	8.3	5.2	2.8	1.5	0	0	0	0	0	0.1	1.8	5.8	25.5
	PRECIPITATION (IN.)	1.41	1.55	2.84	3.81	3.97	4.18	4.37	4.07	3.5	2.52	2.72	2.28	37.22
MOLINE	AVG. MAX. TEMP. (°F)	29.8	35.6	48.3	61.7	73.3	82.7	86.1	83.9	76.5	64.4	48	34.5	60.4
	AVG. MIN. TEMP. (°F)	12.3	18.2	29	39.3	50	59.7	64.5	62.4	53.4	41.6	30.1	18.3	39.9
	SNOWFALL (IN.)	10.2	7.2	4.9	1.3	0	0	0	0	0	0.2	3	8.5	35.3
	PRECIPITATION (IN.)	1.58	1.51	2.92	3.82	4.25	4.63	4.03	4.41	3.16	2.8	2.73	2.2	38.04
MOUNT CARMEL	AVG. MAX. TEMP. (°F)	38	44.1	54.5	65.8	75.9	85.1	88.6	87	80.7	69.6	55.3	43	65.6
	AVG. MIN. TEMP. (°F)	21	24.8	34.5	43.9	54.1	63.2	67.1	64.5	56.5	44.7	35.7	25.5	44.6
	SNOWFALL (IN.)	4.6	3.7	1.4	0	0	0	0	0	0	0.1	0.1	2.5	12.4
	PRECIPITATION (IN.)	2.9	2.73	4.15	4.24	5.12	3.7	4.24	3.61	2.8	3.03	4.19	3.05	43.76

*equivalent to rainfall

ILLINOIS CLIMATE NORMALS 1971–2000

(Data from the Midwestern Regional Climate Center.)

MT. VERNON

CATEGORY	JAN	FEB	MAR	APR	MAY	JUN	JUL	AUG	SEP	OCT	NOV	DEC	YEAR
AVG. MAX. TEMP. (°F)	37	42.8	53.7	64.8	74.5	83.7	87.8	86.3	79.2	68.2	53.9	41.8	64.5
AVG. MIN. TEMP. (°F)	18.8	22.9	32.9	43.2	52.6	62	66.4	63.9	55.5	43.2	34.1	23.8	43.3
SNOWFALL (IN.)	6.4	4.5	1.9	0.4	0	0	0	0	0	0.2	0.7	3.6	17.7
PRECIPITATION (IN.)	2.45	2.69	3.98	4.44	4.58	3.61	3.57	3.27	3.11	2.92	4.37	3.2	42.19

PEORIA

	JAN	FEB	MAR	APR	MAY	JUN	JUL	AUG	SEP	OCT	NOV	DEC	YEAR
AVG. MAX. TEMP. (°F)	30.7	36.6	49.4	62	73	82.2	85.7	83.6	76.7	64.4	48.8	35.5	60.7
AVG. MIN. TEMP. (°F)	14.3	19.7	30.2	40.3	50.8	60.1	64.6	62.6	54	42.3	31.4	20.1	40.9
SNOWFALL (IN.)	8.3	5.6	3.2	1	0	0	0	0	0	0	2.1	7.1	27.3
PRECIPITATION (IN.)	1.5	1.67	2.83	3.56	4.17	3.84	4.02	3.16	3.12	2.77	2.99	2.4	36.03

QUINCY

	JAN	FEB	MAR	APR	MAY	JUN	JUL	AUG	SEP	OCT	NOV	DEC	YEAR
AVG. MAX. TEMP. (°F)	32.7	38.7	50.9	63.1	72.8	81.8	86	84	77.1	65.5	50.2	37.2	61.7
AVG. MIN. TEMP. (°F)	16.7	22	32.3	42.8	53	62.2	66.6	64.3	55.9	44.6	33.2	21.9	43
SNOWFALL (IN.)	7.6	6	2.8	0.8	0	0	0	0	0	0	2.3	4.9	24.4
PRECIPITATION (IN.)	1.36	1.84	3.04	3.79	4.86	3.61	3.84	3.44	3.85	3.21	3.23	2.37	38.44

ROCKFORD

	JAN	FEB	MAR	APR	MAY	JUN	JUL	AUG	SEP	OCT	NOV	DEC	YEAR
AVG. MAX. TEMP. (°F)	27.2	33	45.5	59.1	71.2	79.9	83.1	80.9	73.9	61.8	45.5	32	57.8
AVG. MIN. TEMP. (°F)	10.8	16.3	26.7	36.8	47.9	57.6	62.6	60.9	51.8	40.1	29	16.9	38.1
SNOWFALL (IN.)	10.3	8	5.6	1.4	0	0	0	0	0	0.1	2.6	10.8	38.8
PRECIPITATION (IN.)	1.41	1.34	2.39	3.62	4.03	4.8	4.1	4.21	3.47	2.57	2.63	2.06	36.63

SPRINGFIELD

	JAN	FEB	MAR	APR	MAY	JUN	JUL	AUG	SEP	OCT	NOV	DEC	YEAR
AVG. MAX. TEMP. (°F)	33.1	38.9	51.1	63.4	74.4	83.3	86.5	84.5	78.5	66.6	50.9	38	62.4
AVG. MIN. TEMP. (°F)	17.1	22.2	32.4	42.2	52.7	61.9	66	63.9	55.4	44.4	33.7	22.6	42.9
SNOWFALL (IN.)	7.4	5.8	3.5	0.7	0	0	0	0	0	0	1.6	6	25
PRECIPITATION (IN.)	1.62	1.8	3.15	3.36	4.06	3.77	3.53	3.41	2.83	2.62	2.87	2.54	35.56

WATERLOO

	JAN	FEB	MAR	APR	MAY	JUN	JUL	AUG	SEP	OCT	NOV	DEC	YEAR
AVG. MAX. TEMP. (°F)	37.6	44	54.8	66	75.6	84.4	88.5	86.9	79.9	68.6	54.3	42	65.2
AVG. MIN. TEMP. (°F)	20.3	25.1	35.1	44.6	54.7	63.8	68.1	66.2	58.6	47	36.2	25.1	45.4
SNOWFALL (IN.)	4.7	3	1.9	0.7	0	0	0	0	0	0	1.3	3	14.6
PRECIPITATION (IN.)	2.32	2.4	3.73	4.16	4.04	4.01	4.25	3.13	3.41	3.05	4.21	3.4	42.11

ILLINOIS CLIMATE EXTREMES 1971–2000

(Data from the Midwestern Regional Climate Center.)

CARBONDALE

MAXIMUM (°F)	113 AUGUST 9, 1930
MINIMUM (°F)	-25 JANUARY 11, 1977
RAINFALL (IN.)	6.9 JUNE 17, 2000
SNOWFALL (IN.)	10 FEBRUARY 26, 1979

MT. VERNON

MAXIMUM (°F)	114 JULY 14, 1936
MINIMUM (°F)	-22 FEBRUARY10, 1899
RAINFALL (IN.)	6.17 AUGUST 16, 1946
SNOWFALL (IN.)	14 FEBRUARY 21, 1912

CHICAGO

MAXIMUM (°F)	104 JUNE 20, 1988
MINIMUM (°F)	-27 JANUARY 20, 1985
RAINFALL (IN.)	6.49 AUGUST 14, 1987
SNOWFALL (IN.)	18.6 JANUARY 2, 1999

PEORIA

MAXIMUM (°F)	113 JULY 15, 1936
MINIMUM (°F)	-25 JANUARY 17, 1977
RAINFALL (IN.)	5.52 MAY 18, 1927
SNOWFALL (IN.)	12.2 JANUARY 13, 1979

DANVILLE

MAXIMUM (°F)	112 JULY 14, 1936
MINIMUM (°F)	-26 JANUARY 17, 1982
RAINFALL (IN.)	5.4 AUGUST 4, 1968
SNOWFALL (IN.)	14 FEBRUARY 21, 1912

QUINCY

MAXIMUM (°F)	112 JULY 14, 1954
MINIMUM (°F)	-22 DECEMBER 22, 1989
RAINFALL (IN.)	5.84 JUNE 14, 1950
SNOWFALL (IN.)	10.9 FEBRUARY 25, 1993

GALESBURG

MAXIMUM (°F)	102 JULY 22, 1983
MINIMUM (°F)	-25 JANUARY 10, 1982
RAINFALL (IN.)	7.7 SEPTEMBER 8, 1927
SNOWFALL (IN.)	11 APRIL 11, 1997

ROCKFORD

MAXIMUM (°F)	104 AUGUST 16, 1988
MINIMUM (°F)	-27 JANUARY 10, 1982
RAINFALL (IN.)	5.7 AUGUST 14, 1987
SNOWFALL (IN.)	10.6 DECEMBER 15, 1987

MOLINE

MAXIMUM (°F)	106 AUGUST 18, 1936
MINIMUM (°F)	-28 FEBRUARY 3, 1996
RAINFALL (IN.)	6.21 SEPTEMBER 13, 1961
SNOWFALL (IN.)	16.4 JANUARY 3, 1971

SPRINGFIELD

MAXIMUM (°F)	112 JULY 14, 1954
MINIMUM (°F)	-22 FEBRUARY 26, 1963
RAINFALL (IN.)	5.12 SEPTEMBER 26, 1959
SNOWFALL (IN.)	17 DECEMBER 12, 1972

MOUNT CARMEL

MAXIMUM (°F)	102 AUGUST 1, 1980
MINIMUM (°F)	-19 JANUARY 20, 1985
RAINFALL (IN.)	4.6 JULY 27, 1979
SNOWFALL (IN.)	10 MARCH 20, 1996

WATERLOO

MAXIMUM (°F)	107 AUGUST 21, 1962
MINIMUM (°F)	-18 DECEMBER 22, 1989
RAINFALL (IN.)	7.03 AUGUST 20, 1915
SNOWFALL (IN.)	15 JANUARY 31, 1982

LAST SPRING FROST DATES

	BEFORE APRIL 7
	APRIL 7 – APRIL 14
	APRIL 14 – APRIL 21
	APRIL 21 – APRIL 28
	AFTER APRIL 28

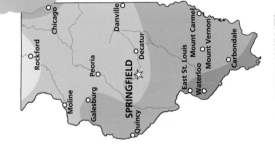

FIRST FALL FROST DATES

	BEFORE OCTOBER 7
	OCTOBER 7 – OCTOBER 14
	OCTOBER 14 – OCTOBER 21
	AFTER OCTOBER 21

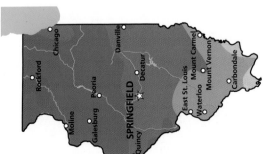

AVERAGE ANNUAL MINIMUM TEMPERATURE

ZONE	TEMP (°F)
4b	-20 to -25
5a	-15 to -20
5b	-10 to -15
6a	-5 to -10
6b	-0 to -5

JANUARY

Now is the time for planning and
dreaming of the distant summer
and the garden yet to be.

JANUARY

1

2

*Instead of chemical de-icers that may
injure surrounding plants, consider
using sand, sawdust or kitty litter
on icy sidewalks and driveways.*

3

4

*Recycle a Christmas tree by cutting off
branches to layer on perennial beds.
Cut the trunk for firewood but
age it for a year.*

*Keep poinsettias blooming by keeping soil
moist and protecting them from cold drafts
or temperatures.*

5

6

7

One of the flowers you might dream of adding to
your garden this spring is the beautiful hybrid tea
'Loving Memory' (*left*). This zone 5 rose will flourish
in most Illinois gardens. Snow on pine (*right*)

J anuary is a fickle month, bringing howling winds and snows or moderate, almost balmy conditions in more southern areas of the state. The freeze-thaw cycle can injure many types of plants. Around the home, watch how snow melts quickly on south-facing surfaces and garden beds but more slowly on the north side. Mulches help moderate temperature swings.

THINGS TO DO

January is one of the hardest months for the garden and the easiest for the gardener.

Wet snow can injure evergreen branches. Use a broom to sweep snow off bent limbs, allowing junipers and other evergreens to rebound to their natural shape. Do not chip at ice; it can break off a limb or ice-encrusted foliage.

Don't forget to top up your bird-feeders regularly. Feeding the birds encourages them to keep visiting in summer when they will help keep your insect pest populations under control.

Snow is a fine natural insulator, so pile extra amounts on garden beds to protect plant roots and provide extra moisture when thaws occur.

8

9

Move houseplants to areas of highest light
in the home—south- or west-facing windows
if possible—but out of the path of cold drafts
or heat ducts.

10

11

Gardening and seed catalogs are great fun
to look through at this time of year.
Also, check out online versions of many
of those same catalogs.

12

13

14

Begonias (*left*) will continue to flower
through winter if brought indoors in
autumn and kept on a sunny windowsill.
Snake plant (*right*)

Choose and order seeds for early starting. Sort through the seeds you have, test them for viability and throw out any that don't germinate or that you won't grow. Trade seeds with gardening friends.

Get lawn mowers and other power tools serviced now. They will be ready for use in spring, and you may get a better price before the spring rush.

Annual poppy seeds are easy to collect and share with friends. There are many color choices available in both single- and double-flowering varieties *(right)*.

Wash houseplant leaves with a light solution of dishwashing detergent to help kill insects as well as to provide a better leaf surface to receive the low light levels of winter. Turn plants to balance their growth habit.

To test older seeds for viability, place 10 seeds between two layers of moist paper towel and put them in a sealed container. Keep the paper evenly dampened but not too wet. Seeds may rot if the paper towel is too moist. Check each day to see if the seeds have sprouted. If fewer than half the seeds sprout, buy new ones.

JANUARY

15

16

17

18

19

20

Water houseplants only as needed. Low light levels and cool temperatures mean little moisture is drawn into the foliage for growth.

The datura (*left*) is an elegant, exotic plant that produces large, downward-facing, aromatic flowers. These tropical plants need to be brought inside for winter. Willow with birdfeeders (*top right*); pines and cedar in winter (*near right*); English ivy topiary (*bottom right*) as a houseplant

Sticky leaves are a sign of insects. Check foliage, especially the undersides of leaves and leaf axils for scale, mealybugs, spider mites or whiteflies.

GARDEN DESIGN

As you look out your windows at the frozen yard, think about what could make your garden look attractive in winter. Features such as birdbaths, ponds, benches, decks and winding pathways improve the look and function of your garden year-round. Persistent fruit, unusual bark and branch patterns, evergreens and colorfully stemmed shrubs also provide winter interest.

Brown, dry leaf edges indicate your houseplants would benefit from higher humidity. If you don't have a humidifier attached to your furnace, acquire a small, room-size humidifier and group plants near it.

JANUARY

21

22

*Winter is a great time to catch up
on reading and planning the upcoming year's
garden. Look at the bones of the garden and
decide what needs to be changed or updated
when spring arrives.*

23

24

25

26

27

Rosehips (*left*), the twisted branches of Japanese
maple and the bright berries of viburnum (*top
right*), the seedpods of amur maple (*center
right*), and the persistent fruit of cotoneaster
(*bottom right*) add interest to the garden in
winter.

Plants that add variety to a winter garden:

- Amur Cherry (*Prunus maackii*): coppery, peeling bark
- Cedar (*Thuja*), False Cypress (*Chamaecyparis*) or Juniper (*Juniperus*): evergreen branches
- Clematis (*Clematis*): fuzzy seedheads
- Corkscrew Hazel (*Corylus*): twisted and contorted branches
- Cotoneaster (*Cotoneaster*): persistent red berries
- Dogwoods (*Cornus*): red, purple or yellow stems
- Highbush Cranberry (*Viburnum trilobum*): bright red berries
- Kerria (*Kerria*): bright green stems
- Maples (*Acer ginnala, Acer palmatum*): attractive bark and branching patterns
- Shrub Roses (*Rosa*): brightly colored hips
- Winged Euonymus (*Euonymus alatus*): corky ridges on the branches

JANUARY

28   29

*Imagine the garden you'd like to have,
and keep this gardening notebook and your
diagrams at hand so you can jot down
ideas as they come to you.*

30   31

*If you notice sloping areas that are eroding,
consider groundcovers as a solution.
Many have tight root systems that will
keep soil from washing away.*

Woody evergreens,
such as cedar (*left*),
upright juniper (*top
right*) and white spruce
(*far right*), add
interesting texture and
rich green color to a
sometimes monotonous
winter landscape.

PROBLEM AREAS IN THE GARDEN

Keep track of these potential problem areas in your garden:

- windswept areas: perhaps a tree, shrub or hedge could be added next summer to provide shelter

- snowfree areas: places where the snow is always quick to melt are poor choices for very tender plants, which benefit most from the protection of the snow

- snowbound areas: places where the snow is slowest to melt provide the most protection to plants but stay frozen longest in spring, making them poor locations for spring-flowering plants

- waterlogged areas: places where water is slow to drain or pools during wet weather are good spots for bog plants and moisture-loving plants

- dry areas: places that rarely get wet or that drain quickly can be reserved for drought-resistant plants.

Spruce are widely grown in Illinois, and new varieties are available almost every gardening season. They are well suited to our winters, and some, such as the Colorado blue spruce (*left*), provide rich blue-green color against brilliant white snow.

FEBRUARY

*The longer days and occasional warm
spells turn our thoughts to the
upcoming gardening season.*

FEBRUARY

1

2

Take a catalog and do the math—you'll save a lot of money by buying seeds and growing them instead of buying plants later.

3

4

Remove dying flowers on plants such as azalea, amaryllis, Christmas cactus and gardenia both for looks and to spur new growth in the plant.

5

6

7

Colorful crabapple trees (*left and top right*) bloom in spring but their equally colorful apples often remain on the tree's branches until late winter. Mugo pines (*bottom right*)

Groundhog Day is a dividing line for gardening enthusiasts. We hope that light shining on those pesky garden varmints signals that there is hope for spring sometime, sooner preferably. Pent-up energy can lead us to start seedlings, to prune out crossing branches in ornamental trees or limbs damaged by winter, or to poke around the mulch looking for the first signs of crocus or glory-of-the-snow (*Chionodoxa*). These activities can help us cope with the dreary weather that's still to come before spring.

THINGS TO DO

February can be relatively laid-back or it can be a planning time that will make way for a smooth and efficient season. Walking the garden can yield a long list of chores to be performed when the weather cooperates.

Cut branches of flowering shrubs, such as forsythia, crabapple and cherry, to bring indoors. Placed in a bright location in a vase of water, they will begin to flower, giving you a taste of spring in winter.

FEBRUARY

8

9

Check for frost heaving of perennials and push them back into the soil. Provide extra mulch to keep them from heaving again.

10

11

Get pots, containers and flats ready for spring by washing thoroughly and rinsing in a 10% bleach solution.

12

13

14

Dianthus (*left*), browallia (*top right*), bellflower (*far right*) and begonia (*near right*) are plants you can start from seed in February.

Start seeds for annuals, perennials and vegetables that are slow to mature. A few to consider are

- Amethyst Flower (*Browallia*)
- Begonia (*Begonia*)
- Bellflower (*Campanula*)
- Geranium (*Pelargonium*)
- Hollyhock (*Alcea*)
- Lady's Mantle (*Alchemilla*)
- Onion (*Allium*)
- Petunia (*Petunia*)
- Pinks (*Dianthus*)

If you are itching to start some seeds this month, consider perennials. They need around 12 weeks to be ready to plant. Most annual flowers and vegetables should be delayed until at least March because they typically need 4–8 weeks to be garden-ready.

FEBRUARY

15

16

Many orchid species bloom in late winter. Moth orchids (Phalaenopsis) will stay in flower for many months if given moderately bright light and semi-frequent feedings.

17

18

Check to see if any of the tubers or bulbs you are storing indoors have started sprouting. Pot them and keep them in a bright location once they do.

Try starting seeds from grapefruit, lime, lemon or oranges—they will grow into handsome foliar houseplants.

19

20

21

Many varieties of dahlia (*left*) can be started from seed in February for transplanting after the danger of frost has passed. Orange trees as houseplants (*top left*); fresh herbs growing in a greenhouse in winter (*center right*); seed tray, pots, soil and spray mister for indoor seeding (*bottom right*)

Prune back winter injury on trees and shrubs before foliage returns and obscures the problem. Prune grapes early in the month to avoid sap 'bleed.'

Check shrubs and trees for storm-damaged branches, and remove them using proper pruning techniques.

Seedlings will be weak and floppy if they don't get enough light. Consider purchasing a fluorescent or other grow light (*above*) to provide extra illumination for them.

STARTING SEEDS

To start seeds you'll need:
- pots, trays or peat pots
- sterile seed-starting mix
- plastic bags or tray covers to keep the seedbed humid
- spray bottle or watering can with sprinkler attachment
- heat mat (optional)

Tips for growing healthy seedlings:
- Transplant seedlings to individual containers once they have three or four true leaves to prevent crowding.
- Space plants so that the leaves do not overshadow those of neigh-boring plants.
- Grow seedlings in moderate tem-peratures away from direct heat.
- Provide air circulation with a small fan to keep foliar diseases from starting.

22

23

As the days get longer, indoor plants may start to show signs of new growth. Increase watering and apply a weak fertilizer (1/4 strength) only after they begin to grow.

24

25

Dormant oil spray breaks insects' life cycles without using pesticides. Use it on many ornamental and fruit trees before they leaf out and when the temperature is above 40° F.

26

27

28

29

The floribunda rose 'Fellowship/Livin' Easy' (*left*) is well known for its reliable vigor, attractive foliage and showy, long-lived blooms. It also makes a great cut flower.

Seed starting tips:

- Moisten the soil before you fill the containers.
- Firm the soil down in the containers, but don't pack it too tightly.
- Leave seeds that require light for germination uncovered.
- Plant large seeds individually by poking a hole in the soil with the tip of a pen or pencil and then dropping the seed in the hole.
- Spread small seeds evenly across the soil surface, then lightly cover with more soil mix.
- To spread small seeds, place them in the crease of a folded piece of paper and gently tap the bottom of the fold to roll them onto the soil (*top right*).
- Mix very tiny seeds, like those of begonia, with very fine sand before planting to spread them out more evenly.
- Plant only one type of seed in each container. Some seeds will germinate before others, and it is difficult to keep both seeds and seedlings happy in the same container.
- Cover pots or trays of seeds with clear plastic to keep them moist (*right*).
- Seeds do not need bright, direct light to germinate and can be kept in an out-of-the-way place until they begin to sprout.
- After germination, and once seedlings start to emerge, moisten the soil with a hand-held spray mister when it begins to dry out.
- Keep seedlings in a bright location to reduce stretching, and remove plastic cover.

To prevent seedlings from damping-off, always use a sterile soil mix, thoroughly clean containers before using them, maintain good air circulation around seedlings and water from the bottom, keeping the soil moist, not soggy.

FEBRUARY

Envision the garden you desire rather than the one you have by sketching a landscape plan. Design your garden beds in a free-flowing pattern and avoid straight lines if you can. Sketch a plan with ideas as simple as containers on a patio or as complex as beds and borders that include fences or raised beds (*opposite*).

N

FLOWERBED

FLOWERING CRABAPPLE

PATIO

HOUSE

FLOWERBED

FLOWERBED

WALKWAY

RED MAPLE

DRIVEWAY

GARDEN PLANNING

- Using graph paper, plot out the existing yard and house. Put in trees, shrubs and other structural elements such as patios and decks. Sketch existing flower and vegetable beds, and orient the sketch to know where the sun will pass from east to west.

- Create a master plan including all projects, then sub-plans so you can stage the work and keep track of changes you want to make each year.

- Make another plan of the vegetable garden, if applicable, to plan and keep track of crop rotations. Also note the height of various crops to keep tall crops from shading shorter ones.

MARCH

Expect the unexpected in March. Our gardens
can be under a blanket of snow one day
and showing the first signs of spring the next.

1

2

Work the vegetable garden as soon
as the soil dries enough to be crumbly.
Fork or till in compost or manure.

3

4

The single most important thing you can do
when planting is to make sure you have the
right plant in the right location.
Consider the mature size of the plant
and its cultural requirements.

Fertilize woody plants before they begin to
make new growth.

5

6

When designing your garden, consider planting a fast-
growing, drought-tolerant elder (*left*). The elder's
showy foliage adds color and texture to a landscape,
and its edible berries can be made into jelly or wine or
left for the birds. Flowering dogwood (*top right*)

7

Early warm spells lure us out to see what's sprouting. Witch-hazel unfolds its spidery flowers, hellebores open from beneath the melting snow and the earliest spring bulbs herald in the much-anticipated spring. Just when we think winter is over, a late snowfall blankets the garden and we go back to planning.

THINGS TO DO

The first few tasks of spring get us out in the garden by late March.

Days can be warm enough for some plants to start sprouting. Keep snow piled on beds or mulches topped up to protect plants from the freezing nights.

Prune red-twig dogwoods (*below*) in early spring for more colorful stems. The river birch (*left*) is heat tolerant, fast growing and resistant to the fatal bronze birch borer.

MARCH

8

9

As the snow melts, it often uncovers items that
should be cleared, such as leaves, sticks,
garbage and pet waste.

10

11

Prune damaged growth off your shrubs. Prune
now to shape late-flowering shrubs (July or
later). Cut back butterfly bush and Russian
sage to 6" to rejuvenate.

12

13

14

As soon as the snow begins to melt
in spring, the leaves of the
bergenia become visible and
are quickly followed by its
pretty magenta flowers (*left*).
Spirea (*top right*); hardy kiwi
(*center right*); climbing
hydrangea (*bottom right*)

Keep off your lawn when it is frozen, bare of snow and/or very wet to avoid damaging the grass or compacting the soil.

Apply horticultural oil (also called dormant oil), used to control over-wintering insects, to trees, shrubs and vines before the buds swell. Follow the directions carefully to avoid harming beneficial insects.

Plants to prune in spring
- False Spirea (*Sorbaria sorbifolia*)
- Hardy Kiwi (*Actinidia arguta*)
- Japanese Spirea (*Spirea japonica*)
- Potentilla (*Potentilla* spp.)
- Red-twig Dogwood (*Cornus alba*)
- Rose-of-Sharon (*Hibiscus syriacus*)
- Yellow or Purple-leafed Elders (*Sambucus*)

MARCH

15

16

Most annual and vegetable seeds can be started indoors. Point to the expected planting date and work back to determine which week to start each variety.

17

18

Begin more frequent watering and diluted fertilization of houseplants that show new growth. Check pots for signs the plant needs repotting.

19

20

21

Bigleaf hydrangea (*left*) is a popular shrub that needs a moist location and protection in some northern areas of the state. If planted early enough in spring, clematis (*top left*) flowers the first summer; daffodils (*far right*); tulips and hostas (*bottom right*)

PLANTING IN SPRING

As March draws to a close, we head into prime planting season. Trees, shrubs, vines and perennials often establish most quickly when they are planted just as they are about to break dormancy. They are full of growth hormones, and they recover quickly from transplant shock.

Avoid using dormant oil on blue-needled evergreens, such as blue spruce. The treatment takes the blue off the existing growth, though the new needles will be blue.

MARCH

22

23

Before doing any digging, call your utility companies to locate any buried wires, cables or pipes to prevent injury and save time and money.

24

25

Don't plant vigorous spreaders in rock gardens with tiny alpine plants or large shrubs right next to walkways.

26

27

28

Rhododendrons (*left*) thrive in acidic soils, which is a problem in alkaline areas of the state. Try little-leaf types or build a special bed using pine bark and needles with compost or peat to create an acidic soil profile with good drainage. Flowering quince (*top right*); goat's beard (*bottom right*)

PLANTING TIPS:

- Work soil when it is neither soggy nor bone dry. Try to work an entire bed before planting—if you plant first and do prep work later, it can injure newly forming roots.
- Heavy spring digging can cause injury. Bend at the knees and lift with the legs, not the back.
- Plant new perennials and woody plants as soon as possible after purchasing to get them started in their new homes. Mail-order plants often come in small pots; repot the plants into larger pots and put in a sheltered location to acclimate them before planting.
- Plants have a better survival rate if planted at the same depth they were in the pot. Trees in particular can die if planted too deeply.
- Plant on an overcast day, or plant early or late in the day. Avoid planting in the heat.
- Remove all potting material and check root mass. Girdling roots should be loosened or scored with a knife to encourage new feeder root growth.
- Plants should be well watered when they are newly planted. Watering deeply and infrequently will encourage the strongest root growth.
- Check the root zone before watering. The soil surface may appear dry when the roots are still moist.

MARCH

29

*If a plant needs well-drained soil
and full sun to thrive, it will be healthiest
and best able to fight off problems in
those conditions. Work with your plants'
natural tendencies.*

30

31

A hardy and prolific bloomer, 'Morden Sunrise'
(*below*) is one of the few yellow shrub roses that
will survive in every corner of the state.

Harden annuals and perennials off before planting them by gradually exposing them to longer periods of time outside. Doing so gives your plants time to adapt to outdoor weather conditions and reduces the chance of transplant shock.

Remove only damaged branches when planting trees or shrubs, and leave the plant to settle in for at least one year before you begin any formative pruning. Plants need all the branches and leaves they have when they are trying to get established.

Trees less than 5' tall do not need staking unless they are in a very windy location. Unstaked trees develop stronger root systems.

staking a tree properly

planting a balled-and-burlapped tree

planting a bare-root tree

APRIL

The snow melts, the garden comes to life.
With all the sprouting and flowering going
on, we know that spring is finally here.

APRIL

1

2

Plant dormant trees, shrubs and vines once the soil can be worked.

3

4

Minimize pollution by having your lawnmower's air filter cleaned as part of a servicing. Make sure to have the blades sharpened.

5

6

7

The columbine (*left*) is a beautiful flower that some say resembles a bird in flight. Its jewel-like colors herald the coming of summer. *Clockwise from top right:* primrose; tulips; lungwort

By making regular trips to the garden center through-out the spring and summer, you'll become familiar with the many plants available and when they are flowering or putting on their best decorative display. The best selection of uncommon annuals and perennials is usually available early.

The warming days can't mask the fact that frosts can still intrude, not to mention a late snow. Bulbs brighten the landscape, wood-land ephemerals make their triumphant appearance and woody plants slowly unfurl their new canopies. There is so much to do to get ready for the planting season that the month typically flies past.

THINGS TO DO
The real gardening work begins—raking, digging, planting and pruning. We begin the hard work that will let us sit back and enjoy the garden once summer arrives.

APRIL

8

9

Remove mulch from perennial beds. Cut back old growth. Trim ornamental grasses to within 6" of the soil line.

10

11

Prune dead wood from roses. Look for green canes and a swelling bud. Cut at a diagonal just beyond this point. Fertilize the plants.

12

13

14

Consider planting daylilies (*left*) this spring. Though each bloom lasts only a day, these lilies are easygoing, prolific and versatile, and come in an almost infinite variety of forms, sizes and colors. Magnolia (*top right*); California poppies (*bottom right*)

Bring garden tools out of storage and examine them for rust or other damage. Clean and sharpen them if you didn't before you put them away in fall.

Store any plants you have purchased or started indoors in as bright a location as possible. You may begin to harden them off by placing them outdoors for a short period each day.

Avoid working soil that is wet. If you have used a heavy mulch, remove it and allow the dark soil to absorb sunlight for some days. Take a handful of soil, squeeze it into a ball, and if it breaks apart easily, the soil is dry enough to dig.

Seeds sown directly into the garden may take longer to germinate than those planted indoors, but the resulting plants, such as poppies (*below*), will be stronger.

APRIL

15

16

Divide perennials that bloom in mid-summer or later, such as asters, daylilies and sedums.

17

18

Cool, wet spring weather can cause some drought-loving plants to rot. Improve soil drainage through the addition of organic matter.

19

20

21

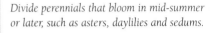

A traditional garden favorite, sweet peas (*left*) are easy to grow from seed in spring. They sprout quickly and have sweetly scented blooms that can be cut often for fragrant indoor bouquets. *Clockwise from top left*: phlox, cabbage, rocket larkspur and nigella can be planted before the last spring frost.

Warming up vegetable beds with row covers allows many plants and seeds to be sown early.

Many plants prefer to grow in cool weather and can be started well before the last frost. These seeds can be planted as soon as the soil can be worked:

- Bachelor's Buttons (*Centaurea cyanus*)
- Cabbage (*Brassica oleracea*)
- Calendula (*Calendula officinalis*)
- California Poppy (*Eschscholzia californica*)
- Godetia (*Clarkia amoena*)
- Kale (*Brassica napus*)
- Love-in-a-Mist (*Nigella damascena*)
- Peas (*Pisum sativum*)
- Phlox (*Phlox drummondii*)
- Poppy (*Papaver rhoeas*)
- Rocket Larkspur (*Consolida ajacis*)
- Spinach (*Spinacea oleracea*)
- Sweet Pea (*Lathyrus odoratus*)
- Swiss Chard (*Beta vulgaris*)

APRIL

22

23

Unpot houseplants and look for root problems: insects, too many roots twisted at the bottom of the rootball; dark areas that may mean rot.

24

25

Take soil samples from several areas of the yard and have them tested. A pH reading of 7 is neutral. Soil with a reading above 7 is alkaline; soil below 7 is acidic.

26

27

28

You can depend on aubrieta (*left*) to put on a great floral show in spring. *Clockwise from top right:* spiral juniper; pompom topiary; formally pruned yew hedge and cedars

PRUNING

Prune trees and shrubs to maintain the health and attractive shape of a plant, increase the quality and yield of fruit, control and direct growth and create interesting plant forms and shapes.

Once you learn how to prune plants correctly, it is an enjoyable garden task. There are many good books available on the topic of pruning. One is listed at the back of this book. If you are unsure about pruning, take a pruning course, often offered by garden centers, botanical gardens and adult education programs.

Don't prune trees or shrubs when growth has started and buds are swelling. Prune before growth starts in spring or wait until plants have leafed out.

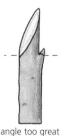

Clockwise from top left: climbing rose with support; an espalier; proper pruner orientation

PRUNING TIPS

- Prune at the right time of year. Trees and shrubs that flower before June, usually on the previous year's wood, should be pruned after they have flowered. Trees and shrubs that flower after June, usually on new growth, can be pruned in spring.

- Use the correct tool for the size of branch to be removed: hand pruners for growth up to ¾" in diameter; long-handled loppers for growth up to 1½" in diameter; or a pruning saw for growth up to about 6" in diameter.

- Always use clean and sharp tools.

- Always use hand pruners or loppers with the blade side towards the plant and the hook towards the part to be removed.

thinning cuts

Thin trees and shrubs to promote the growth of younger, healthier branches. Doing so rejuvenates a plant.

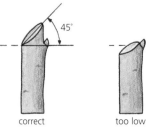

correct   too low   angle too great   too high

45°

When pruning, avoid the following:

- Don't leave stubs. Whether you are cutting off a large branch or deadheading a lilac, always cut back to a stem. Branches should be removed to the branch collar, and smaller growth should be cut back to a bud or branch union. There is no absolute set angle for pruning. Each plant should be pruned according to its individual needs.

- Never use pruning paint or paste. Trees have a natural ability to create a barrier between living and dead wood. Painting over a cut impairs this ability.

- Never try to remove a tree or large branch by yourself. Have some- one help you, or hire a profes- sional to do it.

- Don't cut off the tops of your trees because topping damages tree health and looks ugly.

Always hire an ISA (International Society of Arboriculture) certified professional to remove branches on trees growing near power lines or other hazardous areas, especially if they could damage a building, fence or car if they were to fall. Branches and trees are usually much heavier than anticipated and can do a lot of damage if they fall in the wrong place.

MAY

*The promise of spring is fulfilled
with the blooms of May, and winter
is soon forgotten.*

MAY

As the garden starts to fill in, look for summer-blooming perennials that seem crowded, and then divide or move.

Prune early-flowering shrubs, such as forsythias, after flowering to improve shape or control spread.

The Japanese anemone or windflower (*left*) is an attractive plant at all stages. Some varieties bloom in spring while others reserve their lovely display for late summer and fall. Saucer magnolia (*top right*) flowers in mid- to late spring; the combination of tulips and pansies (*bottom right*) makes an interesting color and height contrast in a spring flowerbed.

May weather can run the gamut, making all planting decisions at-risk propositions. Mother's Day is the bellwether many of us use to signify safety from a late frost. Downstate gardeners can chance planting even earlier. Another test is soil temperature—heat-loving plants like peppers and tomatoes will not begin their spurt until the soil has warmed, so Memorial Day is often used as a safe date for these crops in the northern portion of the state. In general, it's a great month to enjoy the truly diverse display of nature's glory.

THINGS TO DO

A new gardening season awaits, one where we haven't forgotten to weed or water, where all our plants are properly spaced and well staked and where no insects have chewed any leaves. Now is the time to finish tidying up the garden, prepare the garden beds and get the planting done.

MAY

8

9

Begin to harden off any houseplants you plan to move outdoors for summer.

10

11

Work compost into your garden beds and fork them over, removing weeds as you go.

12

13

14

Clematis such as *C.* 'Gravetye Beauty' (*left*) is a popular perennial vine with beautiful, showy flowers in many shapes and sizes. By planting a variety of cultivars, you can have clematis in bloom from spring to fall. *Clockwise from top left:* C. 'Hagley Hybrid'; *C. integrifolia*; *C. viticella* 'Etoile Violette'

Cut back spring bulb flower stalks as flowers fade, but leave the foliage to ripen naturally. If yellowing daffodil leaves annoy you, gather a handful and tie in a loose knot.

Continue to take clippings and dying foliage to the compost pile. Woody material should be chipped or clipped into short segments to decay faster.

Clematis are heavy feeders that need full sun for best flower production. They also like a cool root zone, so plant them where a groundcover will grow around them or mulch heavily.

Accept that grass will not grow everywhere. Grass requires plenty of sun and regular moisture. In some areas, trees and shrubs shade the ground and compete with the grass for moisture, so the soil does not absorb enough water for grass to grow successfully. Use mulch or other groundcovers in areas where you have trouble growing grass. When selecting trees to plant in the lawn, choose ones that will provide only light shade and that will enjoy the plentiful water they will be sharing with the grass, or have a grass-free zone extending from the base of the tree to the dripline.

MAY

16

Plant summer bulbs such as cannas, gladioli, dahlias, tuberous begonias and caladiums. They make great container plants in addition to the flowering border.

17

18

Plant an extra row in your vegetable garden—if your harvest is bountiful, give it to a local food pantry or homeless shelter.

19

20

21

Plant a sunny spring flower such as leopard's bane (*left*) with tulips and forget-me-nots to create a cheerful May display.

It is possible to have a healthy, attractive organic lawn. Grass is an extremely competitive plant, capable of fighting off invasions by weeds, pests and diseases without the use of chemicals. Watering with compost tea is one way to encourage a healthy lawn.

Lawns need very little water to remain green. Watering deeply and infrequently will encourage deep roots that are not easily damaged during periods of drought. Just ¼" of water a week will keep grass alive, and 1" a week will keep it green (*below*).

The average last frost date falls between mid-April in extreme southern Illinois to mid-May in Rockford and areas to its north and west. Schedule your planting by how the spring is progressing—are trees blooming early or late? If you gamble and plant tomatoes in April or early May, you could gain several weeks on when you receive the first harvest. If frost intercedes, have a back-up set of plants or revisit the garden center. Beans (*left*) like warm soil but are likewise worth the early planting gamble.

MAY

22

23

Harvest green onions, lettuce, radishes, peas and spinach from an early planting; thin beets and carrots; plant swiss chard for summer greens.

24

25

As you plant containers, work in a sweet potato vine or licorice plant to spill over the edge, giving the planting a flowing look.

26

27

28

With a wide variety of leaf shapes, sizes and colors, hostas (*left*) can anchor a shade garden and are easily divided early in the season.

TURFGRASS

Well-grown lawns are a sight to behold—bold, green, evenly cut, weed-free. To get to that stage often requires professional help or the use of a range of chemicals that many of us would rather avoid and a power lawn mower, which has come under increasing scrutiny for its pollution emissions. Lawns have their place—they filter pollutants from run-off water, prevent soil erosion, retain moisture, cool the air and give off oxygen. If you're seeking an alternative consider groundcovers or naturalistic plantings—prairies are an Illinois heritage.

Although lawns need a layer of thatch to improve wear tolerance, reduce compaction and insulate against weather extremes, too thick a thatch layer can prevent water absorption, make the grass susceptible to heat, drought and cold and encourage pests and diseases.

May-blooming flowers: (*clockwise from top*) bearded irises bloom in early spring; forget-me-nots flower in spring, set seed and eventually go dormant; rockcress (*Arabis*) and phlox flowers attract bees and butterflies in spring and look exceptional in rock gardens.

29   30

31

Give tomato plants room to grow, whether along the ground, vertically on a stake or inside a cage. If space is an issue, place a large cage in a bed and plant 4–6 plants around the outside edge, then tie up the vines as they grow.

Forget-me-not (*left*), daylily (*top right*) and bergenia (*bottom right*) are easy-to-grow, reliable bloomers and perfect for beginner gardeners.

Here are some tips for maintaining a healthy, organic lawn:

- Aerate your lawn in spring after active growth begins to relieve compaction and allow water and air to move freely through the soil.

- Feed the soil, not the plants. Organic fertilizers or compost encourage a healthy population of soil microbes. These work with roots to provide plants with nutrients and to fight off attacks by pests and diseases. Apply organic fertilizer in late spring after aerating the lawn and in fall just as the grass goes dormant.

- Mow lawns to a height of 2–2¹/₂". If kept this height, the remaining leaf blade will shade the ground, reducing moisture loss, keeping roots cooler, reducing the stress the grass suffers from being mowed and helping the grass out-compete weeds for space and sunlight.

- Grass clippings should be left on the lawn to return their nutrients to the soil and add organic matter. Mowing your lawn once a week or as often as needed during the vigorous growing season will ensure that the clippings decompose quickly.

- Healthy turfgrass out-competes most weeds. Remove weeds by hand. If you must use chemicals, apply them only to the weeds. Chemical herbicides disrupt the balance of soil microbes and are not necessary to have a healthy lawn.

JUNE

The long, warm days
of summer are with us, and the
garden flourishes.

JUNE

Prune back chrysanthemums to encourage bushiness and delay flowering until the proper time in fall. Prune again around July 1st but not after the 4th.

Heat-loving plants such as beans and marigolds will germinate quickly in the warm soil. Direct sow early in June.

Cranesbill geraniums (*left*) are charming late spring perennial flowers with attractive foliage. *Clockwise from top left:* bee balm, flowering tobacco and cleome; water-garden with irises and pots of pansies; a mixed bed of annuals and perennials, including *Salvia farinacea*, coreopsis, petunias, hostas and beebalm; rock garden with lilies and annuals

Remove dead flowers from plants growing in containers. Deadheading encourages more flowering and keeps displays looking tidy.

Early June is a special time in most Illinois gardens. The weather settles somewhat and gardens and lawns are full and lush. Assess what is in bloom now and write down your impressions. Are there too many spring bloomers? Is the color palette in need of an overhaul? Are there not enough tall plants? Likewise, determine where more annual color is needed and make another trip to the garden center for fill-in plants.

JUNE

Prune early-flowering shrubs that have finished flowering to encourage the development of young shoots that will bear flowers the following year.

Watch for insect feeding on foliage, then find out what's causing it before reaching for an insecticide. You may be surprised to find out how many insects are beneficial.

Despite the delicate look of its satiny flowers, godetia (*left*) enjoys the cooler weather of spring and early summer. Plants often die back as the summer progresses. *Clockwise from center right:* black-eyed Susans mixed with purple coneflower; purple coneflower; artemisia

THINGS TO DO

There are always chores to do in June, most of a pleasurable nature. Weeds are prolific, so stay ahead of them at all costs.

Remove the foliage of spring-flowering bulbs as it yellows and dies for both looks and sanitation.

Prune evergreen shrubs early in the month to give them time to recover and send out new growth before autumn. If pruning yew hedges, use an 'A' configuration—prune the bottom wider than the top of the plant to allow light to reach emerging needles.

Apply mulch after the soil warms and before hot/dry weather takes hold. It will hold down new weeds and conserve moisture.

Fertilize roses once a month to keep them vigorous. Old-fashioned roses bloom prolifically now but infrequently over the rest of the summer.

Deadhead perennials to extend the flowering season.

Perennials to pinch back in June:

- Artemisia (*Artemisia* spp.)
- Bergamot (*Monarda didyma*)
- Black-eyed Susan (*Rudbeckia* spp.)
- Catmint (*Nepeta* hybrids)
- Purple Coneflower (*Echinacea purpurea*)
- Shasta Daisy (*Leucanthemum* hybrids)

JUNE

Pull weeds when they are young, before they flower. Once they set seed, you can count on seeing them again next year.

Water transplants regularly until they become established.

Coreopsis (*left*) enlivens a summer garden with its bright yellow, continuous blooms. Shear back in late summer for more flowers in fall. *Clockwise from top right*: abutilon in a container; formal containers with vinca, bacopa, verbena and other annuals; nasturtiums, daisies, geraniums, asparagus ferns and bacopa in a terra-cotta pot.

CONTAINER GARDENING

Most plants can be grown in containers. Annuals, perennials, vegetables, shrubs and even trees can be adapted to container culture.

There are many advantages to gardening in containers:

- They work well in small spaces. Even apartment dwellers with small balconies can enjoy the pleasures of gardening with planters on the balcony.
- They are mobile. Containers can be moved around to take advantage of light or shade and can even be moved into a sheltered location for winter.
- They are easier to reach. Container plantings allow people in wheelchairs or with back problems to garden without having to do a lot of bending.
- They are useful for extending the season. You can get an early start without the transplant shock that many plants suffer when moved outdoors. You can also protect plants from an early frost in fall.

JUNE

Put trailing plants near the edge of a container to spill out and bushy and upright plants in the middle where they will give height and depth to the planting.

Consider mixing different plants together in a container. You can create contrasts of color, texture and habit and give a small garden an inviting appearance.

The flowers of *Salvia farinacea* 'Victoria' (*left*) are a beautiful deep violet blue. They look stunning planted with yellow or orange flowers such as nasturtiums, California poppies or marigolds.

Clockwise from top left: lettuce in a unique tub planter; a deck improved by a vibrant container garden; terracotta pot filled with petunias, dahlias and ornamental millet; marigolds, sweet potato vine and begonias in planters

Gardeners can get over a month's head start on the gardening season by using containers. Tomatoes, pumpkins and watermelons can be started from seed in late March. Planted into large containers, they can be moved outside during warm days and brought back in at night as needed in April and May. This prevents the stretching that many early started plants suffer from if kept indoors for too long before being planted into the garden.

Many houseplants enjoy spending the summer outside in a shady location. The brighter a location you need to provide for your plant indoors, the more likely it is to do well outdoors. When placing plants outside, avoid putting plants in direct sun because they will have a hard time adjusting to the intensity of the light and the lack of light when they are moved back indoors at the end of the summer.

JUNE

Watch closely for early signs of insect and disease problems. Remove diseased plants, look for insect hiding places and destroy.

Petunias (*left*) have gained renewed popularity with Illinois gardeners as new forms and colors have come to the market. Look for the Wave series or the many colors of Supertunias or million bells. Spirea (*top right*) by water feature

Don't have room for a pond with a waterfall? Don't despair. Preformed ponds are widely available in small sizes and container water gardening is gaining appeal. A large pot without drainage holes can be fitted with a circulating pump and a few plants for a patio water feature.

Most perennials, shrubs or trees will require more winter protection in containers than they would if grown in the ground. Because the roots are above ground level, they are exposed to the winter wind and cycles of freezing and thawing. Protect container-grown plants by insulating the inside of the container. Thin sheets of foam insulation can be purchased and fitted around the inside of the pot before the soil is added. Containers can also be moved to sheltered locations. Garden sheds and unheated garages work well to protect plants from the cold and wind of winter.

Prune pines once new growth has fully extended, but while it is still tender. This new growth is called a 'candle' (*right*). Each candle can be pinched back by up to half to two-thirds to encourage bushier growth. Old-wood shoots and branches can be pruned from pine and spruce at their bases.

JULY

The hot, sunny days of July encourage us
to sit back, relax and enjoy all the hard
work we've put into our gardens.

JULY

1

2

Deadhead repeat-blooming annuals and perennials regularly to keep them looking their best.

3

4

Cut flowers to use in fresh arrangements indoors.

5

6

7

'Anisley Dickson' (*left*), better known as 'Dicky,' is a reliable repeat bloomer when planted in full sun. It can produce up to 120 late-summer blossoms in its first season. A riot of phlox, daylilies, yarrow, ageratum and snapdragons (*top right*); Japanese barberry is striking when planted in large groups (*bottom right*).

Flowerbeds have filled in, green tomatoes are on the vine. The season's transplants are established and need less frequent watering. By July, the days are long, warm and humid. The garden appears to grow before your eyes. Some plants can't take the heat and fall dormant while others thrive, filling in the spaces left by the spring-flowering plants.

THINGS TO DO

In the heat of midsummer, we must pay close attention to our watering practices. Remember to water deeply and only as needed. Deep watering done infrequently promotes deeper rooted, more drought-resistant plants than frequent, shallow watering. Quickly check whether your soil needs watering by probing the soil with your fingers to a depth of 2–3".

Water early in the day to minimize potential disease and reduce water lost through evaporation.

Top up water gardens regularly if levels drop because of evaporation.

Thin direct-seeded vegetable crops such as beets, carrots and turnips. Crowded plants lead to poor crops.

Train new shoots of climbing vines such as morning glory, clematis and scarlet runner bean to their supports.

JULY

8

9

*Provide a water source for birds.
They help control insects. Butterflies likewise
need a water source.*

10

11

*Turn the compost pile and when the
compost is ready, add it to your flowerbeds
and vegetable garden.*

12

13

*Take cuttings from perennials
to create new plants.*

14

Annual clary sage, *Salvia viridis,* (*left*) loves sun, and
its brilliantly colored bracts attract butterflies and
hummingbirds to the flowers. Plant it among other
sun-loving annuals and perennials where its bright
whites, pinks and purples will provide bright bursts of
color. *Clockwise from top left:* four-o'clock flower;
portulaca; bachelor's buttons

Use an organic fertilizer on container plants and on garden plants if compost is scarce.

Pick zucchini when they are small. They are tender and tasty and you are less likely to wind up with boxes full of foot-long zucchini to leave on unsuspecting neighbors' front doorsteps. Consider donating extra vegetables to a homeless shelter or food bank, where they will be much appreciated.

Plan to replace fading flowers and vegetables by sowing seeds for a fall display or crop. Peas, bush beans, annual candytuft and lobelia are often finished fruiting or blooming by mid- to late summer, leaving holes in the garden that can be filled by new plants. Seeds for replacement plants can be direct sown or started indoors.

JULY

15

16

Top mulch up if it is getting thin in places in your garden. Mulch protects roots, holds in moisture and helps keep weeds at bay.

17

18

Continue to tie plants to their stakes as they grow.

19

20

Heliopsis (*below*), a native prairie perennial, is easy to grow and tolerates poor conditions, though it thrives in full sun and fertile, moist soil. Its name means 'resembling the sun' and its sun-like blooms make long-lasting cut flowers.

21

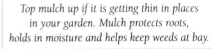

Location is a critical element for the survivability of a plant. Map the sun patterns to determine how sunny or shady a location is for a prospective plant. 'Full sun' on a plant tag means at least 6 hours. If some shade will intervene, it's better after midday—hot afternoon sun damages plants more quickly than morning sun.

GARDEN PROBLEMS

Problems such as chewed leaves, mildews and nutrient deficiencies tend to become noticeable in July when plants finish their first flush of growth and turn their attention to flowering and fruiting.

Such problems can be minimized if you develop a good problem management program. Though it may seem complicated, problem management is a simple process that relies on correct and timely identification of the problem and then using the least environmentally harmful method to deal with it.

Use a mixture of annuals and perennials to create garden rooms that add privacy or create paths through the garden (*above and below*).

JULY

22

23

Heat stress affects containers greatly. Water daily and fertilize as often as weekly with compost tea or diluted liquid fertilizer.

24

25

Cut flowers can be hung upside down in an airy location to dry for winter.

26

27

28

'Cupcake' (*left*) is a delightful miniature rose with a classic hybrid tea shape. It produces an abundance of blooms and is disease resistant. *Clockwise from top left:* deer-pruned cedars; a swallowtail on cherry blossoms; a birdbath in a shade garden.

Garden problems fall into three basic categories:

- pests, including aphids, nematodes and whiteflies, and animals such as mice, rabbits and deer
- diseases, caused by bacteria, fungi and viruses
- physiological problems, caused by nutrient deficiencies, too much or too little water, incorrect light levels and severe exposure.

Choose healthy plants that have been developed for their resistance to common problems and that will perform well in the conditions provided by your garden.

Prevention is the most important aspect of problem management. A healthy garden is resistant to problems and develops a natural balance between beneficial and detrimental organisms.

JULY

The natural pesticide pyrethrin is derived from certain species of chrysanthemums.

Cup-and-saucer vine (*below*) produces sweetly scented flowers that are cream colored when they emerge and turn purple as they age. Ladybug (*top right*), a beneficial insect that feasts on aphids; Dahlberg daisies (*bottom right*)

PEST CONTROL

Correct identification of problems is the key to solving them. Just because an insect is on a plant doesn't mean it's doing any harm.

Chemical pest control should always be a last resort. There are many alternatives that pose no danger to gardeners or their families and pets.

- Cultural controls are the day-to-day gardening techniques you use to keep your garden healthy. Weeding, mulching, keeping tools clean and growing problem-resistant cultivars are a few techniques you can use to keep gardens healthy.

The pesticide industry has responded to consumer demand for effective, environmentally safe pest control products. Biopesticides are made from plant, animal, bacterial or mineral sources. They are effective in small quantities and decompose quickly in the environment. These products may reduce our reliance on chemical pesticides.

- Physical controls are the hands-on part of problem solving. Picking insects off leaves, removing diseased foliage and creating barriers to stop rabbits from getting into the vegetable patch are examples of physical controls.

- Biological controls use natural and introduced populations of predators that prey on pests. Birds, snakes, frogs, spiders, some insects and even bacteria naturally feed on some problem insects. Soil microbes work with plant roots to increase their resistance to disease.

AUGUST

Though the warm weather continues,
the ripening fruit, vegetables and seeds are
signs that summer is nearing its end.

1

2

Reduce fertilizer applications to allow perennials, shrubs and trees ample time to harden off before the cold weather.

3

4

Continue to water during dry spells. Plants shouldn't need deep watering more than once a week at this time of the year.

5

6

7

Verbena (*left*) works well in full sun and can be used as a groundcover, in beds, along borders or in containers.
From top right: geraniums; ripening apples; petunias

The hot and humid days of July blend into August when, with luck, slightly cooler nights arrive toward the end of the month.

THINGS TO DO

We putter about, tying up floppy hollyhock spikes, picking vegetables and pulling the odd weed, but the early summer frenzy is over, and we take the time to enjoy the results of our labors.

Continue to deadhead perennials and annuals to keep the blooms coming.

Harvest the vegetable garden frequently, and look for open places to plant seeds for fall crops. Many summer crops begin to fail. Remove the spent foliage quickly to keep diseases from moving in and contaminating the soil. Consider planting a green manure crop such as alfalfa for open areas—it will enrich the soil for next season. Water with drip irrigation to save water and keep moisture off foliage.

Watch for insect pests—Japanese beetles have become serious pests recently in many Illinois communities. Carry a bowl containing water and dish detergent through the garden and tap the slow-moving beetles off foliage into the bowl.

Pick apples as soon as they are ready, being careful not to bruise the fruit.

AUGUST

8

9

Edge beds and sidewalks to neaten their appearance. A sharp square-bladed spade and/or string-trimmer make the job easier.

10

11

Depending on the size of your perennials, you can divide them using a shovel or pitchfork (for large plants), a sharp knife (for small plants) or your hands (for easily divided plants).

12

13

14

The French marigold (*left*) is just one variety of this popular annual. All marigolds are low-maintenance plants that stand up well to heat, wind and rain.

PLANT PROPAGATION

Now is a good time to divide some perennials and to note which of your plants will need dividing next spring. Look for these signs that perennials need dividing:

- The center of the plant has died.
- The plant is no longer flowering as profusely as it did in previous years.
- The plant is encroaching on the growing space of other plants.

August is a good time to propagate plants. Dividing perennials and gathering seed are great ways to increase your plant collection and to share some of your favorite plants with friends and family.

Plants such as Siberian bugloss (*top*), anemone (*top right*), scabiosa (*center*) and liatrus (*right*) are good plants to divide if you're just starting your perennial collection. They recover and fill in quickly when divided.

AUGUST

16

Gradually move houseplants that have been summering outdoors into shadier locations so they will be prepared for the lower light levels indoors. Make sure they aren't infested with bugs; the pests will be harder to control once the plants are indoors.

Turn the layers of the compost pile and continue to add garden soil, kitchen scraps and garden debris that isn't diseased or infested with insects.

Zinnias (*below*) are easy to grow, come in a rainbow of colors and make long-lasting cut flowers for floral arrangements. *Clockwise from top left:* dianthus, sedum and asters are easy to propagate from stem cuttings.

Perennials, trees, shrubs and tender perennials that are treated like annuals can all be started from cuttings. This method is an excellent way to propagate varieties and cultivars that you really like but that are slow or difficult to start from seed or that don't produce viable seed.

The easiest cuttings to take from woody plants such as trees, shrubs and vines are called semi-ripe, semi-mature or semi-hardwood cuttings. They are taken from mature new growth that has not become completely woody yet, usually in late summer or early fall.

There is some debate over what size cuttings should be. Some claim that smaller cuttings are more likely to root and will root more quickly. Others claim that larger cuttings develop more roots and become established more quickly once planted. Try different sizes and see what works best for you.

AUGUST

Continue watering newly planted
perennials, trees and shrubs.
Water deeply to encourage root growth.

Avoid pruning rust-prone plants
such as mountain ash and crabapple in
late summer and fall because many rusts
are releasing spores now.

You won't need to collect seed from
borage (*left*) because these plants self-
seed profusely and will no doubt turn
up in your garden next spring.
Clockwise from top right: evening
primrose; nasturtiums with creep-
ing Jenny; zinnias

The easiest way to start your seed collection is to collect seeds of annual plants in your own garden. Choose plants that are not hybrids, or the seeds will probably not come true to type and may not germinate at all. A few easy plants to collect from are

- Borage (*Borago officinalis*)
- Calendula (*Calendula officinalis*)
- Coriander (*Coriandrum sativum*)
- Evening Primrose (*Oenothera biennis*)
- Fennel (*Foeniculum vulgare*)
- Marigold (*Tagetes* species and hybrids)
- Nasturtium (*Tropaeolum majus*)
- Poppy (*Papaver rhoeas*)
- Zinnia (*Zinnia elegans*)

Always make cuttings just below a leaf node, the point where the leaves are attached to the stem.

Many gardeners enjoy the hobby of collecting and planting seed. You need to know a few basic things before you begin:

- Know your plant. Correctly identify the plant and learn about its life cycle. You will need to know when it flowers, when the seeds are likely to ripen and how the plant disperses its seeds in order to collect them.
- Find out if there are special requirements for starting the seeds. For example, do they need a hot or cold period to germinate?

Seed areas of the lawn that are thin or dead. Keep the seed well watered while it germinates.

Nasturtiums (*below*) are versatile annuals. Their edible flowers and foliage are attractive additions to baskets and containers as well as to salads. Even the seedpods can be pickled and used as a substitute for capers. *Clockwise from top left:* annual 'Hens and Chickens' poppy seedheads; seedheads of pasque flower; golden clematis flowers and seedheads

Seed collection tips:

- Collect seeds once they are ripe but before they are shed from the parent plant.

- Remove capsules, heads or pods as they begin to dry and remove the seeds later, once they are completely dry.

- Place a paper bag over a seedhead as it matures and loosely tie it in place to collect seeds as they are shed.

- Dry seeds after they've been collected. Place them on a paper-lined tray and leave them in a warm, dry location for one to three weeks.

- Separate seeds from the other plant parts before storing.

- Store seeds in air-tight containers in a cool, frost-free location.

- Plant short-lived seeds right away if propagation information mentions planting freshly ripened seed.

Don't collect seeds or plants from the wild because wild harvesting is severely depleting many plant populations. Many species and populations of wild plants are protected, and it is illegal to collect their seeds.

Collecting and saving seeds is a time-honored tradition. Early settlers brought seeds with them when they came to North America and saved them carefully each fall for the following spring.

SEPTEMBER

Though we cling tenaciously to any summer weather that lingers, there's no denying that fall is upon us.

SEPTEMBER

1

2

Pinch off the tops of tomato plants to concentrate energy on ripening fruit.

3

Shop for colorful fall ornamentals, such as pansies, chrysanthemums, flowering cabbage and flowering kale. Garden centers are stocked up for a new season.

4

5

6

7

Strawflower (*left*), ornamental grasses (*top right*), amaranthus (*center right*), and *Caryopteris* with ornamental grass (*bottom right*) can be harvested now for dried flower arrangements.

L abor Day is the mythical dividing line marking the end of summer, but it often is an idyllic time for weather across the state. Nights are cooler, days are noticeably shorter, the sun less intense. In the garden, hues begin to change as the brighter colors of summer give way to the many yellow-based mum colors and the blue-purples of asters.

THINGS TO DO

Autumn is a good time to do projects: build a gazebo, dig a (another?) pond, tear out and reseed a troubled lawn or set up a greenhouse to continue gardening through winter.

Scout out bargains at garden centers. Trees and shrubs are marked down and often perennials can be purchased at a fraction of their spring prices. Knock plants out of pots to examine roots—if they are too potbound, seek other plants.

Consider starting some herb seeds now. You can plant them in pots and keep them in a bright window so you'll have fresh herbs to add to soups and salads over winter. Moving herb plants in from outdoors is also possible, but the plants often have a difficult time adapting to the lower light levels indoors.

SEPTEMBER

8

9

Harvest potatoes and garlic after their tops have died. Plant garlic cloves and cover with mulch.

10

11

Continue to water the garden during dry spells. Consistent watering in fall helps prepare plants for winter.

12

13

14

Clockwise from top left: the fall colors and features of Virginia creeper, burning bush, full moon maple and ginkgo. Lilies (*left*) are long-lived, easy-to-grow perennials. They look superb in floral arrangements combined with flowers such as baby's breath.

Pull weeds before they set seed to prevent even more weeds next summer.

Now is the perfect time to renovate spent areas of the lawn. Work the soil and add starter fertilizer before seeding. Cover seeds and water lightly and daily for 3–4 weeks. Overseeding is one way to thicken thin lawns. Keep grass well watered and fertilized during this time. Pull any weeds revived by the cooler weather.

Changing colors are a highlight of the upcoming season. Bright reds, golds, bronzes and coppers seem to give warmth to a cool day. The display doesn't have to be reserved for a walk in the park. Include trees and shrubs with good fall color such as the ones listed here in your garden:

- Burning Bush (*Euonymus alatus*)
- Cotoneaster (*Cotoneaster* spp.)
- Maples (*Acer* spp.)
- Virginia Creeper (*Parthenocissus quinquefolia*)
- Witch-hazel (*Hamamelis* spp.)

SEPTEMBER

15

16

Set up birdfeeders and begin to fill them regularly. Add a suet feeder to attract a wider range of birds.

17

18

Most houseplants fare well outdoors for much of the month. All Ficus species should be brought in as they are affected by dramatic shifts in temperatures and humidity.

19

20

The cheery golden marguerite daisy (*below*) forms a tidy mound that works wonderfully in both formal and informal garden settings. *Clockwise from top left:* Asiatic lily 'Electra'; tulips; black-eyed Susan; alliums

21

Begin to plant bulbs for a great display next spring. Alliums, crocuses, daffodils, muscaris, scillas and tulips are just a few of the bulbs whose flowers will welcome you back into the garden next year.

Spring-flowering perennials such as candytuft and primroses will be a delightful sight come March and April and can be planted now.

For vivid color from summer through fall, a continuous blooming perennial such as black-eyed Susan can't be beat.

SEPTEMBER

22

23

When planting bulbs, consider covering the bed with chicken wire or cloth mesh to discourage squirrels from plundering your treasure. Fertilize with bonemeal.

24

25

Insects inevitably hide in houseplants. Wash thoroughly or spray with insecticidal soap before bringing the plants indoors.

26

27

28

Echinacea purpurea (*left*), commonly called purple coneflower and used as a popular herbal cold remedy, is a long-blooming, drought-resistant perennial. Its distinctively cone-shaped flowers look good in fresh and dried floral arrangements.

CREATING WILDLIFE HABITAT

The rapid rate of urban sprawl has led to the relentless expansion of large cities and a loss of habitat for wildlife. Our gardens can easily provide some of the space, shelter, food and water that wildlife needs. Here are a few tips for attracting wildlife to your garden:

- Make sure at least some of the plants in your garden are locally native. Birds and small animals are used to eating native plants, so they'll visit a garden that has them. When selecting non-native plants for your yard, choose those that wildlife might also find appealing, such as shrubs that bear fruit.
- Provide a source of water. A pond with a shallow side or a birdbath will offer water for drinking and bathing. Frogs and toads eat a wide variety of insect pests and will happily take up residence in or near a ground-level water feature.

This page: Garden features such as birdbaths, birdfeeders and tall, flowering perennials such as bergamot, coneflower and yarrow attract wildlife to your yard.

- A variety of birdfeeders and seed will encourage different species of birds to visit your garden. Some birds will visit an elevated feeder, but others prefer a feeder set at or near ground level. Fill your feeders regularly, especially when natural food sources are scarce. Birds appreciate a reliable food source.

SEPTEMBER

29

30

The zinnia (*below*) is named after Johann Gottfried Zinn (1727–59), a German botany professor who started growing these South American flowers from seed in Europe. *Clockwise from top left:* birdfeeder; *Aphrodite fritillary* on bergamot; sunflower; Japanese maple

- Butterflies, hummingbirds and a wide variety of predatory insects will be attracted if you include lots of pollen-producing plants in your garden. Plants such as goldenrod, comfrey, bergamot, salvia, Joe-Pye weed, black-eyed Susan, catmint, purple coneflower, coreopsis, hollyhock and yarrow will attract pollen lovers.

- Shelter is the final aspect to keeping your resident wildlife happy. Patches of dense shrubs, tall grasses and mature trees provide shelter. As well, you can leave a small pile of twiggy brush in an out-of-the-way place. Nature stores and many garden centers sell toad houses and birdhouses.

Inevitably squirrels and chipmunks will try to get at your birdfeeders. Instead of trying to get rid of them, why not leave peanuts and seeds out for them as well? Place them near a tree, where they can easily get at them. If you have a large spruce tree, they will eat the seeds out of the cones. Leave cones out with the other food offerings. The little cone scales that are left when they are done make great mulch for the garden or can be used to prevent slipping on icy walks and driveways.

OCTOBER

This month marks the inevitable end
of summer. Frosts and falling leaves
remind us that winter is not far off.

OCTOBER

1

2

Continue to plant bulbs. The roots they send out in the warm autumn soil will help their flowering show next spring.

3

4

As leaves begin to fall, keep them from accumulating on turf areas. Wet leaves can smother grass. Rake them off before mowing or mow over them and let the shredded remains settle into the turf.

5

6

7

If the first frost hasn't yet arrived and your apples are still on the tree (*left*), now is the time to harvest them. However, some varieties taste better after the first frost. *Clockwise from top right:* luminous fall leaves; a bountiful harvest of carrots; endearing teddy bear sunflowers

Our gardens will be vigorous early this month but by Halloween, only hardy bloomers and some late fall vegetables will still be going strong. Frost will greet us in the morning at some point in most parts of the state, and if we're really unfortunate, a dusting of snow might arrive. Adios to the annual garden.

THINGS TO DO

October is the time to finish tidying up and putting the garden to bed for another year.

Harvest any remaining vegetables. Soft fruit such as tomatoes and zucchini should be harvested before the first frost, but cool weather vegetables such as brussels sprouts, cabbage, carrots and turnips can wait a while longer because they are frost hardy.

Unless your plants have been afflicted with some sort of disease, you can leave faded perennial growth in place and clean it up in spring. The stems will collect leaves and snow, protecting the roots and crown of the plant over the winter.

OCTOBER

8

9

Stop fertilizing houseplants. Growth slows in the lessened light of autumn.

10

11

Clean the area around plants that can be affected by leaf diseases—roses and apple trees especially. Plant debris also affords a home for overwintering insects. Compost or discard diseased foliage, shred leaves and return to flowerbeds as mulch.

12

13

14

The serviceberry (*left*) is a small tree that bears white flowers and edible red berries in spring and lovely orange-red foliage in fall. It requires little maintenance and does quite well near water.

Fall is a great time to improve your soil. Amendments added now can be worked in lightly. By planting time next spring, the amendments will have been further worked in by the actions of worms and other soil microorganisms and by the freezing and thawing that takes place over winter.

Dig up dahlias, canna lilies, begonias, caladium and gladioli before a freeze. Clean off soil and store in a cool, dark location. Dahlia tubers and begonia corms should be packed in slightly moist peat moss; gladioli bulbs can be stored in a paper bag.

Local farmers' markets are often the best places to find a wide variety of seasonal produce and flowers (*above and below*).

OCTOBER

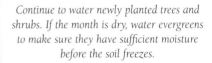

15

16

Continue to water newly planted trees and
shrubs. If the month is dry, water evergreens
to make sure they have sufficient moisture
before the soil freezes.

17

18

Faded annuals and vegetables can be pulled
up and added to the compost pile.

19

20

21

Honeysuckle vine (*left*) flowers from late summer to
fall frost and attracts hummingbirds. Composting
(*far right*); delicious fruits and vegetables harvested
from the garden (*near right*)

COMPOSTING

One of the best additives for any type of soil is compost. Compost can be purchased at most garden centers, and many communities now have composting programs. You can easily make compost in your own garden. Though garden refuse and vegetable scraps from your kitchen left in a pile will eventually decompose, it is possible to produce compost more quickly. Here are a few suggestions for creating compost:

- Compost decomposes most quickly when there is a balance between dry and fresh materials. There should be more dry matter, such as chopped straw or shredded leaves, than green matter, such as vegetable scraps and grass clippings.
- Layer the dry and the green matter and mix in some garden soil or previously finished compost. This step introduces decomposer organisms to the pile.

OCTOBER

Pull up hot pepper plants if frost is imminent, bring them inside and hang upside down to dry for winter use.

Pick pumpkins, acorn squash and spaghetti squash before frost and cure them for winter use in a cool, frost-free location. Or carve the pumpkins for jack-o-lanterns!

Yarrow's showy, flat-topped flower-heads (*left*) provide months of continuous color in summer and the seedheads persist into winter.

- Compost won't decompose properly if it is too wet or too dry. Keep the pile covered during heavy rain and sprinkle it with water if it is too dry. The correct level of moisture can best be described as that of a wrung-out sponge.
- To aerate the pile, use a garden fork to poke holes in it or turn it regularly. Use a thermometer with a long probe attached, similar to a large meat thermometer, to check the temperature in your pile. When the temperature reaches 160° F, turn the pile.
- Finished compost is dark in color and light in texture. When you can no longer recognize what went into the compost, it is ready for use.
- Compost can be mixed into garden soil or spread on the surface as a mulch.

Images of fall: ripening cherry tomatoes (*top left*); juicy clusters of vine-ripened grapes (*top*); tasty corn on the cob fresh from the garden (*above*). Many gardeners find fruiting plants to be decorative as well as useful.

OCTOBER

29

30

31

Clean the vegetable garden. Tomato vines can leave disease spores if not removed. If you have green tomatoes, place in a brown paper bag with an apple to trigger ripening.

Sunflowers (*below*) are synonymous with fall for many gardeners. Their bold yellow, seed-filled flowerheads celebrate the harvest season and provide treats for the birds. Viburnum's fall berries (*right*) add color and attract songbirds.

Before adding any amendments to your soil, you should get a soil test done. Simple kits to test for pH and major nutrients are available at garden centers. More thorough tests can be done. Consult your local cooperative extension for more information. These tests will tell you what the pH is, the comparative levels of sand, silt, clay and organic matter and the quantities of all required nutrients. The tests will also tell you what amendments to add and in what quantities to improve your soil.

There are other good amendments for soil, depending on what is required:

- Gypsum can be mixed into a clay soil along with compost to loosen the structure and allow water to penetrate.
- Elemental sulphur, peat moss or pine needles added on a regular basis can make an alkaline soil more acidic.
- Calcitic or dolomitic limestone, hydrated lime, quicklime or wood ashes can be added to an acidic soil to make it more alkaline.

Sunflowers (*above*) and other cut flowers can be found in abundance in farmers' markets throughout the state. Use them for fresh or dried table arrangements, or press them for winter crafts.

NOVEMBER

Branches lie bare, dry flowerheads sway in the breeze and excited birds pick brightly colored fruit from frost-covered branches.

NOVEMBER

Plant newly purchased amaryllis bulbs
and begin watering. They will bloom
in time for the holidays.

If you have healthy willows, dogwoods,
Virginia creeper or evergreens, cut a few
branches to use in Christmas wreaths.
Store in a cool place until needed.

Annual coreopsis (*left*) self-seeds, so it may pop
up from year to year in the same area if left to
its own devices.

D espite a few teasing days of warmth, the weather usually heads downhill in November. Flowers like pansies keep blooming, even under a light blanket of snow, until the ground starts to freeze. Snow can be expected in most areas of the state but it often doesn't accumulate.

THINGS TO DO

Leaf removal is still around in most locales. While many municipalities cart away bagged leaves, resourceful gardeners know these morsels can continue to contribute once shredded or composted.

Harvest any remaining vegetables. Root vegetables, such as carrots, parsnips and turnips, and green vegetables, such as cabbages and broccoli, store well in a cool place, and their flavor is often improved after a touch of frost.

The garden can be quite beautiful in November, especially when persistent fruit becomes more visible on branches (*below*) or after a light dusting of snow or frost (*right*).

NOVEMBER

8

9

*Clear away tools, hoses and garden furniture
before the snow flies so they won't be
damaged by the cold and wet weather.*

10

11

*Cut back perennials to 2–3" and remove the
foliage, especially if diseases were a
problem. Mulch after the soil freezes.*

12

13

14

The beautiful hybrid tea rose
'Rosemary Harkness' (*left*)
produces fragrant orange-yellow
double blooms from summer to
autumn. Like other tender hybrid
teas, it should be protected from
winter weather.

The richly colored rosettes of ornamental kale (*right*) are reminiscent of roses such as 'Hénri Martin' (*above*); mulched strawberry (*center right*); colorful fall maple leaves (*bottom*)

Prepare hybrid tea and other semi-hardy roses for winter before the ground freezes. Mound dirt up over the base and cover with mulch, or cover it with a cardboard box, open the top and fill around the plant with loose, quick-drying material, such as sawdust, shredded leaves or peat moss. Hold the box in place with a heavy rock on top when you are done.

Avoid completely covering perennials with mulch until the ground freezes. Mound the mulch around them (*above*) and store some extra mulch in a frost-free location to add once they are frozen. If you pile the mulch in the garden, you may find it has also frozen solid when you want to use it.

NOVEMBER

A warm spell may cause spring bulbs
to send up shoots, especially grape hyacinth.
This rarely harms the bulb, but mulch
the bed if you are worried.

Fill birdfeeders regularly. Many bird species
prefer to eat at ground level, so scatter some
seeds beneath a tree, or wait for the
inevitable littering as birds knock seeds
from above-ground feeders.

Pieris (*left*) is a beautiful plant all year long. It provides colorful new growth in spring and summer and
flowers from late winter to mid-spring. *Clockwise
from top left:* black-eyed Susan; hens and chicks;
lilac; hollyhocks

If an area of your garden always seems dry, consider a xeriscape planting in that area. Many plants are drought resistant and thrive even in areas that are never watered. Black-eyed Susan, yucca, cosmos, hollyhock, jack pine, lilac, potentilla, sedum and yarrow are just a few of the many possibilities for a dry section of the garden.

Now that you've had the chance to observe your garden for a growing season, consider the microclimates and think about how you can put them to good use. Are any always quick to dry? Do some areas stay wet longer than others? What area is the most sheltered? Which is the least sheltered? Cater your plantings to the microclimates of your garden.

NOVEMBER

After raking and once the lawn is dormant, apply an organic fertilizer. If you haven't needed to mow in a couple of weeks, it is probably sufficiently dormant.

Cut branches of evergreens, collect pine cones and prune back grape vines to provide materials for home-made wreaths or swags for the holidays.

Flowers such as marsh marigolds (*left*), irises (*top and far right*), daylilies (*center right*) and ligularia (*bottom right*) work well in damp areas of the garden because they prefer moist growing conditions.

BOG GARDENING

Turn a damp area into your own little bog garden. Dig out a damp area 18–24" below ground level, line with a piece of punctured pond liner and fill with soil. The area will stay wet but still allow some water to drain away, providing a perfect location to plant moisture-loving perennials. A few to consider are

- Astilbe (*Astilbe* x *arendsii*)
- Cardinal Flower (*Lobelia* x *speciosa*)
- Doronicum (*Doronicum orientale*)
- Goatsbeard (*Aruncus dioicus*)
- Hosta (*Hosta* hybrids)
- Iris (*Iris ensata, Iris siberica*)
- Lady's Mantle (*Alchemilla mollis*)
- Ligularia (*Ligularia dentata* and *wilsoniana*)
- Marsh Marigold (*Caltha palustris*)
- Meadowsweet (*Filipendula rubra* and *ulmaria*)
- Primrose (*Primula japonica*)
- Rodgersia (*Rodgersia aesculifolia*)

NOVEMBER

Get a hint of spring by growing fragrant bulbs. Paperwhite narcissus are easy to grow and require no soil—just water. For something even more exotic, grow freesias. They need bright light and cool temperatures.

Clockwise from top left: Oregon grape holly; rose-of-Sharon 'Woodbridge'; pieris; yew hedge

Rodgersia (*left*) bears bold foliage and fluffy flower plumes in mid- to late summer. It does best in a site sheltered from strong winds and extreme weather. Rodgersia plants prefer moist soil and require winter protection in colder parts of the state.

It is possible to grow out-of-zone plants. Reserve the warmest, most sheltered area of the garden for plants not considered fully hardy. Pieris, Oregon grapeholly and *Caryopteris* may survive in a suitably sheltered location.

If you have a very exposed area in your garden, you can find plants that will do well there, or you can make a planting that will shelter the area. A hedge or group of trees or shrubs will break the wind and provide an attractive feature for your garden.

DECEMBER

Already summer seems far away. Ghostly forms and dashes of color are all that remain to inspire us until spring.

DECEMBER

1

2

As the soil begins to freeze, apply mulches. Unshredded leaves can blow away.

3

4

Wash hand tools thoroughly and apply a light coat of oil to guard against rust. Sharpen shovels and all pruning tools before storing.

5

6

7

Holly (*left*) makes an attractive addition to fresh winter arrangements. To keep it looking its best, keep the cut ends consistently moist. Dogwoods and evergreens (*top and far right*) add interest to your garden in winter; decorative Christmas peppers are ideal for holiday color indoors (*bottom right*).

If rabbits and mice are a problem in your garden, you can protect your trees and shrubs with chicken wire. Wrap it around the plant bases and higher up the tree or shrub than you expect the snow to reach.

The garden begins its winter display of colorful stems, peeling bark, branches with persistent fruit and evergreen boughs. With a bit of luck, snow begins to pile up on garden beds, covering withered perennials and shrubs and clinging to evergreen branches. Winter arrives, hopefully with a natural white blanket for the holidays, giving our gardens a new and wonderful perspective.

THINGS TO DO

Outdoor chores are there for the doing, but it's more pleasurable to fuss over plants in the confines of home.

We forget the downside of snow. It is a fine insulator, but if trampled, it can lead to plant suffocation. It dusts shrubs but can weigh down and break branches of evergreens.

If the soil is still not frozen, water evergreens and shrubs. Evergreens lose water through their needles all winter.

DECEMBER

8

9

Move clay and concrete pots and statues
into a protected location to prevent them
from cracking over winter.

10

11

Chinese evergreen, peace lily, schefflera,
calathea and prayer plant are a few
examples of houseplants that tolerate low
light levels.

12

13

14

Poinsettias (*left*) add rich color and beauty to our
homes during the dark days of December. *Clockwise
from top left:* bonsai; *Cattleya* orchid; *Miltonopsis*
orchid; spider plant

HOUSEPLANT CARE

There's a whole new world of gardening that is practiced year-round, but especially in winter—indoor gardening. There are easily as many interesting plants available for the indoor gardener as there are outdoor plants. They are no harder to grow and give pleasure every day of the year.

Just as you did for the garden outdoors, match your indoor plants to the conditions your home provides. If a room receives little light, consider houseplants that require very low light levels. Plants that like humid conditions, such as African violets, ferns and philodendrons, may do best in your bathroom where water from showering and the toilet bowl maintain higher moisture levels than in any other room. Plants that tolerate or prefer dry air, such as cacti and palms, will grow well with no added humidity.

15

16

Wait for the ground to freeze up before covering or wrapping tender shrubs and evergreens to ensure that all growth has slowed for winter.

17

18

Bright-light houseplants include asparagus ferns, begonias, cacti and succulents such as aloe, hens and chicks, jade and clivia.

African violets are the most popular houseplant. They are easy to propagate by teasing away side shoots as they develop.

19

20

Although orchids are reputed to be difficult and needy, some orchids such as the moth orchid *Phalaenopsis (left)* are easy to grow on a windowsill. There are many thousands of species of orchids in an amazing array of sizes, shapes, colors and fragrances. Pearl plant and tiger jaws (*center right*); Japanese sago palm (*bottom right*)

21

There are three aspects of interior light to consider: intensity, duration and quality. Intensity is the difference between a south-facing window with full sun and a north-facing room with no direct sunlight. Duration is how long the light lasts in a specific location. An east-facing window will have a shorter duration of light than a south-facing window. Quality refers to the spectrum of the light. Natural light provides a broader spectrum than artificial light.

Watering is a key element to houseplant care. Over-watering can be as much of a problem as under-watering. As you did with your garden plants, water thoroughly and infrequently. Let the soil dry out a bit before watering plants. Some plants are the exception to this rule. Find out what the water requirements of your houseplants are so you will have an idea of how frequently or infrequently you will need to water.

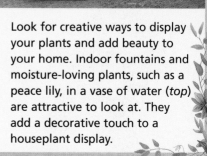

Look for creative ways to display your plants and add beauty to your home. Indoor fountains and moisture-loving plants, such as a peace lily, in a vase of water (*top*) are attractive to look at. They add a decorative touch to a houseplant display.

DECEMBER

22

23

Plant your Christmas tree this year. Balled-and-burlapped or container trees are available. Build a stand for the rootball, keep them indoors no longer than 7 days, plant them in a hole you prepared in autumn and enjoy them in the landscape for many years.

24

25

Don't be upset if your Christmas cactus blooms earlier than its naming. If it is truly happy, it will rebloom in early spring.

26

27

Houseplants allow us to grow exotic-looking specimens that remind us of the tropics. Try red ginger, ti logs, plumeria or coffee plants. Specialty catalogs or online resources can get you started.

28

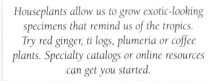

English ivy (*left*) that you've grown outdoors all summer can be brought indoors and kept as a houseplant in winter. Succulent and cacti display (*top right*); snake plant (*bottom right*), a striking, long-lived indoor plant

Houseplants generally only need fertilizer when they are actively growing. Always use a weak fertilizer to avoid burning the roots. Never feed plants when they are very dry. Moisten the soil by watering and then feed a couple of days later.

When repotting, go up by only one size at a time. In general, the new pot should be no more than 2–4" larger in diameter than the previous pot. If you find your soil drying out too frequently, then you may wish to use a larger pot that will stay moist for longer.

Houseplants are more than just attractive—they clean the air in our homes. Many dangerous and common toxins, such as benzene, formaldehyde and trichloroethylene are absorbed and eliminated by houseplants.

Here are a few easy-to-grow, toxin-absorbing houseplants:

- Bamboo Palm (*Camaedorea erumpens*)
- Chinese Evergreen (*Aglaonema modestum*)
- Dragon Tree (*Dracaena marginata*)
- English Ivy (*Hedera helix*)
- Gerbera Daisy (*Gerbera jamesonii*)
- Peace Lily (*Spathiphyllum* 'Mauna Loa')
- Pot Mum (*Chrysanthemum morifolium*)
- Snake Plant (*Sansevieria trifasciata*)
- Spider Plant (*Chlorophytum comosum*)
- Weeping Fig (*Ficus benjamina*)

DECEMBER

Plants can be grouped together in large containers to more easily meet the needs of the plants. Cacti can be planted together in a gritty soil mix and placed in a dry, bright location. Moisture and humidity-loving plants can be planted in a large terrarium where moisture levels remain higher.

A bouquet of cheerful gerberas and painted daisies (*below*) will brighten a drab winter day and remind you of summer, when these flowers were growing in your garden. Fiddle leaf fern, tricolor dracaena and snake plant (*top left*); burro's tail (*top right*)

Keep in mind that many common houseplants are tropical and dislike hot, dry conditions. Most houseplants will thrive in cooler, moister conditions than you will provide in your home. Always turn your thermostat down at night and provide moist conditions by sitting pots on pebble trays. Water in the pebble tray can evaporate but won't soak excessively into the soil of the pot because the pebbles hold it above the water.

There's nothing like treating yourself to a bouquet of fresh flowers (*above*) when you're feeling the doldrums of winter. Many beautiful varieties are available. Watch for some of the more exotic plants from South America and Australia at grocery stores and florist shops.

RESOURCES

All resources cited were accurate at the time of publication. Please note that addresses, phone numbers, websites and e-mail addresses may change over time.

BOOKS

Aldrich, William and Don Williamson. 2003. *Perennials for Illinois*. Lone Pine Publishing, Edmonton, Alberta.

Aldrich, William and Don Williamson. 2003. *Annuals for Illinois*. Lone Pine Publishing, Edmonton, Alberta.

Aldrich, William and Don Williamson. 2004. *Tree and Shrub Gardening for Illinois*. Lone Pine Publishing, Edmonton, Alberta.

Armitage, Allan M. 2000. *Armitage's Garden Perennials A Color Encyclopedia*. Timber Press, Portland, OR.

Bergmann, Craig (Ed.). 2001. *Midwestern Landscaping*. Sunset Books Inc., Menlo Park, CA.

Brenzel, Kathleen N. (Ed.). 1997. *National Garden Book for the U.S. and Canada*. Sunset Books Inc., Menlo Park, CA.

Brickell, Christopher, T.J. Cole and J.D. Zuk (Eds.). 1996. *Reader's Digest A–Z Encyclopedia of Garden Plants*. The Reader's Digest Association Ltd., Montreal, PQ.

Brickell, Christopher and David Joyce. 1996. *Pruning and Training*. Dorling Kindersley, London, England.

Bubel, Nancy. 1988. *The New Seed-Starters Handbook*. Rodale Press, Emmaus, PA.

Courtier, Jane and Clarke, Graham. 1997. *Indoor Plants: The Essential Guide to Choosing and Caring for Houseplants*. Reader's Digest, Westmount, PQ.

DeVore, Sheryl and Steven D. Bailey. 2004. *Birds of Illinois*. Lone Pine Publishing, Auburn, WA.

Duggan, Laara K. 1996. *The Best Flowers for Midwest Gardens*. Chicago Review Press. Chicago, IL.

Duggan, Laara K. 1998. *The Best Plants for Midwest Gardens*. Chicago Review Press. Chicago, IL.

Eder, Tamara. 2001. *Animal Tracks of Illinois*. Lone Pine Publishing, Edmonton, Alberta.

Ellis, B.W. and F.M. Bradley, eds. 1996. *The Organic Gardener's Handbook of Natural Insect and Disease Control*. Rodale Press, Emmaus, PA.

Heintzelman, Donald S. 2001. *The Complete Backyard Birdwatcher's Home Companion*. Ragged Mountain Press, Camden, ME.

Hill, Lewis. 1991. *Secrets of Plant Propagation*. Storey Communications Inc., Pownal, VT.

Hillegass, Linda. 2000. *Flower Gardening in the Hot Midwest*. University of Illinois Press, Urbana and Chicago, IL.

McHoy, Peter. 2002. *Houseplants*. Hermes House, New York, NY.

McVicar, Jekka. 1997. *Jekka's Complete Herb Book*. Raincoast Books, Vancouver, BC.

Merilees, Bill. 1989. *Attracting Backyard Wildlife: A Guide for Nature Lovers*. Voyageur Press, Stillwater, MN.

Robinson, Peter. 1997. *Complete Guide to Water Gardening*. Reader's Digest, Westmount, PQ.

Royer, France and Richard Dickinson. 1999. *Weeds of the Northern U.S. and Canada*. The University of Alberta Press and Lone Pine Publishing, Edmonton, AB.

Thompson, P. 1992. *Creative Propagation: A Grower's Guide*. Timber Press, Portland, OR.

ONLINE RESOURCES

All Organic Links. The global resource for organic information.
http://www.allorganiclinks.com/

Attracting Wildlife to your garden.com. How to make your backyard inviting to compatible and beneficial creatures.
www.attracting-wildlife-to-your-garden.com

Birding.com. Maps, birding information and recommended hot spots for birding throughout Illinois.
http://www.birding.com/wheretobird/Illinois.asp

Butterflies of Illinois. Photos and descriptions of butterflies native to Illinois.
http://www.npwrc.usgs.gov/resource/distr/lepid/bflyusa/il/toc.htm.

Chicagoland Gardening. Articles, advice and information specific to gardening in Illinois.
www.chicagolandgardening.com

Compost Guide. Instructions, articles and guidelines for successful composting in your own backyard.
http://compostguide.com/

Friendship Gardens. Gardening events throughout the state.
www.friendshipgardens.com/illinois.htm

Garden Time Online. Over a thousand free online gardening resources.
www.gardentimeonline.com/illinois.html

Horticultural, Gardening Societies and Organizations. Links to most garden societies throughout the USA.
http://mel.lib.mi.us/science/gardsoc.html

Illinois' Best Plants. Searchable plant database, zone maps and resource lists to help Illinois gardeners find the most suitable plants for their gardens.
http://bestplants.chicago-botanic.org.

I love gardens. Comprehensive listing of gardens to visit throughout Illinois.
www.ilovegardens.com

Northern Gardening Forum. List of gardening forums for northern USA.
www.northerngardening.com/cgi-bin/ultimatebb.cgi

P. Allen Smith. A multifaceted gardening website hosted by garden expert P. Allen Smith, including tips, reports and a newsletter.
http://www.pallensmith.com/

Prairie Wildflowers of Illinois. Information about wildflowers that grow throughout the state and various flora regions.
http://www.shout.net/~jhilty/plant_index.htm

Rain Barrel Guide. How and why to collect rain water for your garden.
http://rainbarrelguide.com/

The Virtual Birder. Includes rare bird alerts, Illinois birding links, resources and a list of birding organizations throughout the state.
www.virtualbirder.com:80/vbirder/real-birds/rbas/IL.html

Turf Resource Center and The Lawn Institute. The latest data regarding turfgrass.
www.LawnInstitute.com

University of Illinois Extension Master Gardener. Program information, contacts and calendars for current and future Master Gardeners.
http://www.extension.uiuc.edu/mg/

University of Illinois Extension Horticulture and Home Garden. Lawn and garden programs for home gardeners
http://www.extension.uiuc.edu/home/homelawn.html

SOIL TESTING FACILITIES
Alvey Laboratory
1511 E. Main St.
PO Box 175
Belleville, IL 62221
618-233-0445
email: alveylab@aol.com

GMS Laboratory
23877 E. 00 North Rd.
PO Box 61
Cropsey, IL 61731
309-377-2851
email: steffen@gmslab.com

Greene County Farm Bureau Soil Testing Laboratory
319 6th St.
Carrollton, IL 62016
217-942-6958

KSI Laboratories
202 S. Dacey Dr.
Box 497
Shelbyville, IL 62565
217-774-2421 or 217-854-2571

Mississippi Valley Soil Testing Lab
1074 Broadway
Hamilton, IL 62341
217-847-3539
email: mvsoil@adams.net

Mowers Soil Testing Plus, Inc.
117 E. Main
PO Box 540
Toulon, IL 61483
309-286-2761

Northern FS Inc.
Soil Testing Laboratory
20048 Webster Rd.
DeKalb, IL 60115
815-756-2739

Southern Illinois Farm Foundation
Soil Testing Laboratory
PO Box 335
Vienna, IL 62995
618-658-2871

Sparks Soil Testing Service
Box 841
Lincoln, IL 62656
217-735-4233
email: sstlinfo@aol.com

HORTICULTURAL SOCIETIES

American Horticultural Society
7931 East Boulevard Dr.
Alexandria, VA 22308
1-800-777-7931
http://www.ahs.org
email: sdick@ahs.org

National Garden Clubs, Inc.
4401 Magnolia Ave.
St. Louis, MO 63110
314-776-7574
http://www.gardenclub.org/
email: headquarters@gardenclub.org

Garden Clubs of Illinois
117 Adell Place
Elmhurst, IL 60126-3301
630-617-9269
http://www.gardenglories.org/
http://www1.math.luc.edu/~pschwal/gci/
email: gardenclubsill@aol.com

Illinois Native Plant Society
Forest Glen Preserve
20301 E. 900 North Rd.
Westville, IL 61883
http://www.inhs.uiuc.edu/inps
email: ilnps@aol.com

GARDENS TO VISIT

Lincoln Memorial Garden and Nature Center
2301 East Lake Shore Dr.
Springfield, IL 62707
217-529-1111
www.lmgnc.com

Alwerdt's Gardens
1 mile S. of I70 on US 128 S. of Altamont
Altamont, IL 62411
618-483-5798
www.altamontil.net/alwerdt.htm

Anderson Japanese Gardens
318 Spring Creek Rd.
Rockford, IL 61107
815-229-9390
www.andersongardens.org

Anna Bethel Fisher Rock Garden
Nelson Park
Nelson Park Blvd. and Lake Shore Dr.
Decatur, IL 62521
217-422-4911

Austin Gardens
N. of Lake St. on Forest Ave.
Oak Park, IL
708-383-0002

Butterworth Center and Deere-Wiman House
1105 8th St.
Moline, IL 61265
309-765-7970
www.butterworthcenter.com

Cantigny Botanical Gardens
1 South 151 Winfield Rd.
Wheaton, IL 60187-6097
630-668-5161
www.cantignypark.com

Chicago Botanic Garden
1000 Lake Cook Rd.
Glencoe, IL 60022
847-835-5440
www.chicagobotanic.org

Garfield Park Conservatory
300 North Central Park Ave.
Chicago, IL 60624-1996
312-746-5100
http://www.garfield-conservatory.org

Klehm Arboretum and Botanic Garden
2701 Clifton Ave.
Rockford, IL 61102
815-965-8146
www.klehm.org

Lincoln Park Conservatory and Gardens
2400 North Stockton Dr.
Chicago, IL 60610
312-742-7736
http://www.chicagoparkdistrict.com/

LinMar Gardens
504 South Prospect
Galena, IL 61036
815-777-1177

Longview Park Conservatory
18th Ave. and 17th St.
Rock Island, IL 61201
309-788-7275
www.rigov.org/citydepartments/parks/
parkinfo.html

Luthy Memorial Botanical Gardens
Glen Oak Park
2218 North Prospect Rd.
Peoria, IL 61603
309-686-3362
www.peoriaparks.org/luthy/luthymain.html

Mari-Mann Herbal Farm
St. Louis Bridge Rd.
Decatur, IL 62521
217-429-5400
www.marimann.com

Mabery Gelvin Botanical Garden
North Route 47
Mahomet, IL 61853
217-586-3360
www.ccfpd.org/gardens.htm

National Shrine of Our Lady of the Snows
442 South De Mazenod Drive
Belleville, IL 62223-1094
618-397-6700
http://www.snows.org/

Oak Park Conservatory
615 Garfield Street
Oak Park, IL 60304
708-386-4700
http://www.visitoakpark.com/index.cfm

Quad City Botanical Center
2525 4th Ave.
Rock Island, IL 61201
309-794-0991
www.qcgardens.com

Rockome Gardens
125 N. County Rd., 425 E.
Arcola, IL 61910
217-268-4106
www.rockome.com

Scovill Home and Oriental Gardens
Scovill Park
55 South Country Club Rd.
Decatur, IL 62521
217-421-7435

The Morton Aboretum
4100 Illinois Rte. 53
Lisle, IL 60532-1293
630 -968-0074
www.mortonarb.org

Timber Ridge Gardens
201 South Elizabeth-Scales Mound
Elizabeth, IL 61028
815-858-3740

Washington Park Botanical Gardens
PO Box 5052
2500 South 11th St.
Springfield, IL 62705
217-753-6228
http://www.springfieldparks.org/garden/
default.htm

ACKNOWLEDGMENTS

We would especially like to thank our
fellow garden writers Alison Beck and Laura Peters
for their many contributions and discussions.

We are grateful to photographers Tamara Eder, Tim Matheson
and Robert Ritchie, and to the many people who opened their
gardens for us to photograph. Special thanks to the Chicago
Botanic Gardens and Morton Arboretum (Illinois); Barbara
and Douglas Bloom, Thea and Don Bloomquist and
Cranbrook Gardens (Michigan); and the International Rose
Test Garden (Oregon) for kindly allowing us to photograph
their plants and gardens.

We would also like to thank Shane Kennedy, Nancy Foulds,
editor Sandra Bit and book designer and Master Gardener
Heather Markham. Thanks also to Gerry Dotto for the cover
design and to Ian Sheldon for the lovely corner flourishes
that grace the pages. Others helped in various ways,
close-cropping photos and providing stylistic solutions,
and we thank them all.

Cover page photos:
January—spruce bough
February—crabapple branches
March—tulips
April—primroses and tulips
May—apple blossoms
June—hosta
July—shrub rose 'The Fairy'
August—dahlias
September—viburnum
October—pumpkins
November—hoarfrost at sunset
December—poinsettias